A Very British Subject

By the same author:

Fourteen Ninety Two: The Year and the Era

The Burning Bush: Antisemitism and World History

Baku to Baker Street (with Flora Solomon)

Weizmann: Last of the Patriarchs

The Letters and Papers of Chaim Weizmann (General Editor)

The Essential Chaim Weizmann (Editor)

Another Time, Another Voice

A Peculiar People: Inside the Jewish World Today

Road to Jerusalem

Ben-Gurion of Israel

Prime Minister David Ben-Gurion and the author at the Israel Embassy in London, 1960

A Very British Subject

Telling Tales

BARNET LITVINOFF

VALLENTINE MITCHELL
LONDON · PORTLAND, OR.

First published in 1996 in Great Britain by
VALLENTINE MITCHELL & CO. LTD
Newbury House, 900 Eastern Avenue, London IG2 7HH

and in the United States of America by
VALLENTINE MITCHELL
c/o ISBS, 5804 N.E. Hassalo Street, Portland, Oregon 97213–3644

Copyright © Barnet Litvinoff 1996

British Library Cataloguing in Publication data
Litvinoff, Barnet
   A very British subject : telling tales
   1. Litvinoff, Barnet 2. Jewish children – England – London –
   Biography 3. World War, 1939–1945 – Personal narratives,
   British 4. Jewish authors – England – London – Biography
   I. Title
   941'.082'092
   ISBN 0 85303 293 9

Library of Congress Cataloging in Publication data
A catalog record for this book is available
from the Library of Congress

ISBN 0 85303 293 9

All rights reserved. No part of this publication may be reproduced in any form or by any means, electronic, mechanical, photocopying, recording or otherwise, without the prior permission of Vallentine Mitchell & Co. Ltd.

Typeset by Regent Typesetting, London
Printed by Redwood Books, Trowbridge, Wilts.

Contents

List of Illustrations	vii
1 A Passage to Russia	1
2 In the Buildings	17
3 Linsi	36
4 Dunkirk on my Mind	48
5 The Cruise of the *Orduña*	56
6 A Blind Date	79
7 The Little Woman and the Great Big Army	87
8 A.W.O.L.	105
9 France at Sea	116
10 Biting the Apple	123
11 God's Footstool	133
12 One Danubian Summer	159
13 Connecting Life-lines	187

List of Illustrations

Frontispiece

Prime Minister David Ben-Gurion and the author at the Israel Embassy in London, 1960

Between pages 10 and 11

1. Rosa Litvinoff in the early 1920s in London's East End

2. Rebecca Roytman, Rosa's friend, in the early 1920s

3. Alec Roytman of Odessa, a soldier in the army of Tsar Nicholas

4. At Bethnal Green Primary School in 1928; the author is holding the class sign

Between pages 50 and 51

5. Alfred, Emanuel and Barnet Litvinoff, 18 December 1940

6. Pinkus Litvinoff, 1942

7. Sylvia Litvinoff in the British Army in 1942, before her husband's capture in the Western Desert

8. The author, just disembarked from the troopship *Orduña* in Ismailya, July 1941

1 • A Passage to Russia

Leaden and chill the morning was as always, but this was not to be a September day like any other. Not for Maksim Litvinoff, anyhow. He would not be taking his usual route in the eight o'clock gloom to the Mile End Road, sandwiches squeezed into his coat pocket, to begin another ten-hour shift head down among the damp Yorkshire worsteds and sizzling steam clouds at Mr Cohen's upstairs workroom in Sidney Street. It might have been the Sabbath, starting the morning without encountering Mr Cohen's red eyes swollen behind those pebble glasses. Only this was Tuesday, not Saturday.

As to a pleasant lemon-tea interlude at Goide's Whitechapel café, its welcoming tables covered in triangular-patterned oil cloth, for a cosy discussion about the war, and socialism, and the riches of the Rothschilds – forget it, Maksim told himself. And that applied also to an evening given over to a hand of *klobiosh*, ha'penny a game. This Tuesday was going to be different.

It was the day Maksim Litvinoff rose specially early, took a hurried wash at the communal sink on the landing of his Stepney tenement, and held out his hands towards Rosa, the wife brought all the way from Russia, to receive a double supply of sandwiches – two cheese, two herring.

A man of few words, Maksim exchanged glances with Rosa and stared into whatever space was available for staring in the room, most of which was surrendered to its iron bedsteads (one large for three infants, one small for two parents), and turned towards the door.

So much in England still puzzled him. What cosmic happenings, for example, had drawn such important attention to his humble self? Who would be disturbed if he did not go as commanded? Would the war's end be delayed? Would 'Loy' George take the matter up? No, he daren't stay for yet another day pressing trousers at Cohen's. Though why not, Maksim wasn't exactly sure.

He carried a suitcase of sorts, closed tight with string, the catches being unpredictable. It contained a pair of shoes, a change of clothing, and a group photograph of the family. Euston Station was a long way away, a bus journey in fact. Could be an hour. What bus did they say? The 'twenty-tree', past Aldgate Church towards Holborn, then along the 'Grayzing' Road to 'Kins' Cross. Twopence early workman's to 'Kins' Cross, and you walked the last little stretch. Well, he'd see the others, and follow them. Following people had long been Maksim Litvinoff's usual procedure. To obtain work as a trousers-presser he had shadowed a basting-hand he overheard making an arrangement with old man Cohen outside the Garment Workers Union off Black Lion Yard.

Maksim, more often called Max by his crowd, drifted rather than walked towards the door. Gently, he closed it behind him so as not to wake Pinny, whose life was still counted in months – fifteen, and Manny, two and a half, sleeping beside Abie, big boy Abie, four-years old bless him. Rosa, well filled out, expected her fourth in November. Would Max be back in London by then? It was another of the many questions he could not answer this autumnal morning in 1917.

Now he carefully descended the bare wooden stairs to avoid the cats, anxious lest he disturb the neighbours or arouse the fates still further. Chance had done mischief enough already, sending him so early to Euston Station, and a train journey that would begin the long road back to Russia. Rosa returned to the urgencies of her own day. Pinny was stirring. Her youngest would need changing.

The knowledgeable reader will require an explanation at this point, for the name Maksim Litvinoff would shortly become familiar, even famous, to students of current affairs. It proclaimed the identity of a revolutionary who in those days likewise resided in London, though in a better neighbourhood. This Litvinoff represented the Russian Bolsheviks scheming that precise moment to oust Alexander Kerensky and the bourgeois reactionaries of the Provisional Government in Petrograd so as to establish the world's first Communist régime. An educated man, one day he would be regarded as a great Foreign Commissar, with his slogan 'Peace is indivisible'. A Jew from Bialystok (hardly a Russian town, more rightly in despised Poland), he had assumed the name unbeknownst to the trousers-presser in order to elude the curiosity of the Russian secret police. Ours was the authentic Litvinoff, born with the name in Odessa. He had nothing to conceal; unless, that is, secret agents hovered around Goide's café and overheard the seditious discussions there.

Our Maksim had arrived in England uninvited, possibly unwanted, in 1913 with his pregnant Rosa. He was not educated. But then, neither was he illiterate. In Odessa, before coming to rest in a tailoring workshop, he had earned his keep as a book-keeper in a grain warehouse by the Black Sea. He knew of no grain warehouses in London, and in any case his English extended to just a few necessary words: please, thank you, a glass of tea with a roll and butter, where is the toilet? That kind of thing. Nevertheless, trousers pressing too was skilled work, though you didn't need to be a genius.

Admittedly, when the war broke out anyone could find a job in the East End of London. The master tailor failing to secure a contract to sew uniforms must have been non-existent. Impossible. Trousers ironed smooth by Max covered many a soldier for whom there would be no homecoming from the Somme. In his way, Max also played his part for the glorious victory 'Loy' George said was assuredly on its way.

Renown lay ahead for his namesake, the educated one. Spokesman of Lenin and Trotsky, jovial tribune injecting much needed sparkle at international conferences, he was destined to earn three inches, as much as Herbert Hoover, thirty-first President of the United States, in the *Penguin Dictionary of Twentieth Century History*; more than Vincent Massey,

A Very British Subject

Governor-General of Canada, though naturally less than Lloyd George, who merited a generous six inches. On the other hand our Maksim Litvinoff, while being primarily responsible for this story, will never be heard of again, by anyone.

From Euston Station he would disappear for ever, lost somewhere in the miasma called the Union of Soviet Socialist Republics – possibly dead, after some heroic stand in the vanguard of the Red Army against the forces of reaction; or renewed after a fashion, perhaps producing more children with another Rosa. Who knows, even changing his identity also, to live on as Commissar of Tailoring in Uzbekistan or Outer Mongolia! It's a provocative thought. Whatever transpired, he would be lost for all eternity to Rosa and her little ones, to Mr Cohen's ironing-table, and to the great metropolis of London. So what impelled him to depart? Who sent him?

High politics, the relationship between trusted allies at a critical moment during the war to end all wars, was responsible for causing Maksim Litvinoff to change direction and board the number twenty-three to Euston. In August 1914, the English, Scots and Irish left towns and villages throughout the kingdom and flocked to the call, which eventuated in an early grave for many of them as the Germans pressed unrelentingly across Belgium and France. With August 1915 the tragedies multiplied: a great Russian army smashed by Field Marshal von Mackeson, débâcle in the Dardenelles, Serbia defeated, and thousands more willing young men left dying or maimed at Ypres.

But in the East End of London life went on: all those tailors and bagel vendors and furniture-makers sleeping in their comfortable Whitechapel beds beside wives pregnant or pregnant-to-be, disturbed only occasionally by the odd Zeppelin raid. Foreigners.

If asked, they described themselves as Russians, though they detested their native heath and had fled from it. They breathed the free, democratic air of England, refraining however from defending this country in its hour of peril. Their gentile neighbours waved the white feather at them and hurled epithets.

Russians? They were just plain Yiddishers, their neighbours said, and did you ever see one of them carry a pick and shovel, let alone a rifle?

They remained unmoved. This was not their war, they protested. It was Britain's war, it was a capitalist war, it was Russia's war. Russia's war? May the Tsar perish! He oppressed the Jews. As far as Whitechapel was concerned the Kaiser was welcome to all the Russias.

August 1916 and the Turks, it was said by accident, captured a great British army in Mesopotamia. Again, largely by understandable error, Britain failed to sink the German navy at Jutland. Kitchener, the War Minister, drowned in the North Sea, and food began disappearing from the shops. The British grew embittered. The struggle hungered for more soldiers, and more, and still more. In Parliament the Home Secretary, a regular busybody named Herbert Samuel, introduced a conscription law. He declared that too many healthy young men were evading their duty. He did not exclude those in the East End, crowded into their tenements and labouring in their sweatshops. Incredible to relate, this Samuel was himself a Jew, though with such Jews in the government who needed a Torquemada? Apparently you were now compelled to go, whether the nation's ordeal stirred your conscience or not.

Or had you? This conscription business was a British law applying to the English, the Scots and the Irish. Maksim Litvinoff, aged about 29, now reminded himself, together with thousands like him, of certain advantages accruing from his Russian nationality. He was a refugee from persecution, and wasn't Britain proud of its reputation as a haven?

Even then he wasn't idle. Who could deny his was an honest, useful job, pressing those khaki trousers for Mr Cohen at eight miserable pence a pair? Let them leave him in peace. (This wasn't entirely his rationalisation; he learned the logic of it at Goide's earnest debating ground, over innumerable glasses of tea.)

Unhappily, the argument ignored the mood of the British people. They didn't particularly care for the Jews, but were totally fair-minded towards such problems as repopulating the trenches on the Western Front. A perfect command of English was not vital in holding the line. An able-bodied man was no less so for being circumcised. This pernicious idea caused an agitation beginning with a whisper and developing into a crescendo. Why must our boys die to protect those alien skins? The *Jewish Chronicle*, worse than any *goy* newspaper with a banner strung across its Finsbury office declaring 'England Has Been All She Should To The Jews, The Jews Will Be All They Can To England', took up the cry, condemning their unheeding co-religionists as 'slackers and shirkers', and worse. Spoiling for blood.

Herbert Samuel kept on about it. Take the king's shilling, he urged. England will be grateful and grant you citizenship after the war. (Oh yes, you should live so long!) It's your war too, Russia is our gallant ally. Samuel sent a man to Bloom's Corner, the open-air forum in Brick Lane, to make recruiting speeches. An indignant group left their regular table at Goide's café to hustle him out of the district. They chased the man and his soap box round Whitechapel, bellowing slogans from the writings of Tolstoy and Kropotkin and inviting Herbert Samuel and the entire Whitehall clique of warmongers to kiss their anarchist arse. One of the hecklers came all the way from neutral New York, passage paid by the Workers' Socialist League, to inspire the waverers.

True, a few cowards slunk away and joined up. Actually, they could state a case. 'Don't forget', they said, 'Turkey is also an enemy, and at present the Turks rule in Palestine. But when they are defeated the British will give it to us, to make a Jewish country again.' That old story! For centuries people made generous promises to restore Palestine to the Jews. The trouble was, the promises came from those who didn't own Palestine to give. As a matter of fact not too many Jews were so keen to have it.

Maksim Litvinoff looked perplexedly from the anarchists to the patriots all through 1916, and half way into 1917. He was a slow mover, and pictured himself trundling through Flanders

A Passage to Russia

in a pair of trousers 32 inches round the waist which he had personally ironed, wondering at the tolerance of sergeant-majors should he fail to comprehend such commands as 'Form Fours!' and 'Advance!'. He thought of the pork he would have to consume, and so decided to do nothing. Not that he made the decision consciously, after balanced deliberation. His friend Alec Roytman the furniture-maker was doing nothing, and Hymie Plotkin, the french polisher who never settled up after a game of *klobiosh*. Nor were countless others. Max merely emulated their inertia.

The year 1917 brought the great German submarine offensive and the slaughter of Passchendaele. Max was on his way to his pressing table in Sidney Street when the postman handed him a buff envelope. On His Majesty's Service. Alec the furniture-maker received one from his postman simultaneously, as did Hymie the french polisher, as well as many more Russian subjects following a life of peace and procreation in the back streets of Stepney and Whitechapel. The envelope contained a solemn message:

> Take notice that facilities have been provided for you to return to Russia under the Military Service (Convention with the Allies) Act, and in order to avail yourself of them you must be at Euston Station, Platform 14, on Tuesday, September 25th at 8.30 am. Not more than two packages of combined weight of not more than 50 pounds can be taken, and each package must have a label attached with the words 'Russian Convention' and the name and serial number of the owner clearly written on them. You are not allowed to take with you letters, English gold or intoxicating liquor. You are advised to take food for the railway journey.
>
> If you fail to avail yourself of this opportunity to return to Russia the necessary steps to enforce your liability to serve in the British army will be taken as soon as possible.

At Goide's and other haunts along the Whitechapel Road, in a hundred workshops punctuating the radials extending from

A Very British Subject

Aldgate Church, and wherever *klobiosh* was helping an evening to while itself away in a ghetto front room, they laboured over the prose of His Majesty's letter, and took a philosophic view of its portent. So what was terrible about returning to the homeland for a period, till the fuss was over? One could see parents again, and have news of brothers and cousins, and walk the familiar streets of Pinsk and Riga and Odessa.

Why not enjoy another taste of real *borsch* in a country where at least you understood the language, and knew how to arrange a few things, maybe get lost? Why rush into uniform over here, to offer yourself up to the Germans on the Western Front, when the Eastern Front was so far away, involving much waiting about at railway stations, not to mention ships to take you across the North Sea? Russia was a continent, it would not be easy to find an army to join, and in the meantime you *lived*.

Hence the trail of tailors and furniture-makers, bagel vendors and sundry stall-holders, together with odd-job men and some with no jobs at all (like the synagogue idlers who said a memorial prayer for your dear departed at sixpence a time) beating a path to Euston – among them Alec and Hymie and Max. Alec and Hymie, with most of the others, would return one day, but Maksim Litvinoff might have travelled via 'Grayzing' Road and 'Kins' Cross to another planet.

When at length they were rounded up for deportation – an ugly term, but accurate – the Provisional Government of Alexander Kerensky was in its Petrograd death throes. The hour now belonged to Lenin, and that other Maksim Litvinoff who was the London spokesman of a Communist government struggling to maintain its authority, patch a treaty with the Germans, feed its people, organise a currency, bring its own Thomasovitch Atkinskys home, and destroy the counter-revolutionaries. Quite an agenda. It left neither time, nor inclination, nor purpose, to put all those returnees from England into uniform, or even to track them down as they spread across an empire rent to tatters by occupation, civil war and hunger.

A Passage to Russia

Rosa Litvinoff, formerly Michaelson, had by some mysterious tribal mechanism (not love, surely?) been matched in 1912 at the age of 19 to her Max in Odessa. She was the eldest of a large family so off they went, like a million or so before them and hundreds of thousands afterwards – fully a third of the Jews of Russia – in search of a life in the western world free from religious discrimination and lack of opportunity.

Mostly the emigrants, once arrived at Hamburg or Rotterdam, had the five pounds necessary for a steerage passage across the Atlantic. It required at least a modicum of foresight, not to mention a degree of determination, and probably a relative already ensconced in the New World – all lacking in the case of Max – to complete the hazardous journey. Almost everyone hoped to finish up in America, the *goldener medina* as it was called in Yiddish, though with each emigration wave a few stragglers were left by the wayside. Needless to say, Rosa and her husband were among the stragglers.

In their case they were carried westward along fortune's stream into Austria-Hungary, with a sojourn in Vienna. There they might have tarried for ever but for the insistence of the local Jewish gentry to keep them on the move. Accommodated for a few nights in a grim hostel, courtesy of the local charitable organisations generous with the funds provided by the Barons de Rothschild and de Hirsch, and they had to be on their way. Jewish philanthropy towards the needy among their people in those days was guided by one rule: help them to disappear. Turning up as they did without notice, weighed down with their clumsily-tied bundles, the refugees would be received by the good Jewish burghers of Budapest, Vienna and Berlin with some distaste. They looked so out of place, so *foreign* in these civilized cities, and never more so than to those comfortably settled for as long as a generation – long enough to assume the air of an 'establishment', as they say. The sight of the newcomers revived memories of their own earlier odyssey, to arouse a disagreeable sensation of insecurity. Feed them? Of course! Help with their documentation at customs sheds and police departments? Naturally, they were fellow-Jews. But, above all, see them through the ticket barriers at railway termini and seaports so that someone else with a kind Jewish heart, at the next staging post, could take over. And the best of luck.

Vienna, Berlin, Brussels all did their duty towards Max and Rosa. At length, by a process of blind man's buff enacted on an inter-territorial scale, availing themselves of every form of transportation including river craft and shanks's pony, they found themselves in Antwerp. It could happen to anybody. The attractive Flemish city rang with the hubbub of transients so eager to put Europe behind them it had developed an industry second only in importance to diamond-cutting: travel agencies. But Max and Rosa had no business with them, even the honest ones, for they had run out of money. So once again they came within the aegis of the Jewish institutions, and the measured benevolence which could bed them down temporarily and arrange the small charity of a short Channel crossing.

Among those similarly placed were Alec Roytman and his wife. Alec transpired to be a *landsmann*, that is, he was likewise a native of Odessa. He had lingered two years in Vienna before moving on, time enough to do his mite for the Austrian population explosion by producing two sons.

A subtle transformation had by this time developed in the relationship between Max and Rosa. She had accompanied her husband in the fond belief that men understood the world. But their travels had revealed Max's limitations in this respect. He was not the monarch of all he surveyed, as husbands were purported to be. Rosa discovered at every stage that unless she took a hand in their destiny they would be jostled into some obscure backwater of Central Europe for ever. Max's initiative had been oozing away ever since their departure from Odessa. Now Rosa looked upon him and observed that it had given out. If he was her compass, it had lost its needle. Though in one respect he justified himself. He had found a *landsmann* – not particularly prosperous, for Alec was likewise stuck in

1. & 2. Rosa Litvinoff (top left) in the early 1920s and her friend Rebecca Roytman (top right), in London's East End

3. Alec Roytman of Odessa, a soldier in the army of Tsar Nicholas

4. At Bethnal Green primary school in 1928; the author is holding the class sign

Antwerp without the means for a transatlantic voyage, but a *landsmann* nevertheless.

Alec might be described as the antithesis of Max. The crucial difference lay rooted in his vocation. He was 'in the furniture', not 'in the tailoring'. That alone bespoke a different attitude to life, and a superior vitality. The tailoring confined you to upstairs airless rooms in artificial light, but furniture men pushed heavily-loaded barrows along cobbled streets, thus developing their muscles and their thirst. They laboured in workshops opening on to wind-swept yards and could breathe a natural atmosphere, albeit permeated by animal smells and clouded with sawdust. Even the most inexperienced among them possessed his own kit of tools, for no one would lend a beginner a smoothing plane or a spokeshave, whereas the tailor carried nothing but a pair of scissors.

In the furniture trade you raised your voice, to exhort a carthorse or command an apprentice. Saw, hammer, drill, they made man's music, while the scissors, the sewing-machine, the steam of the flat-iron, all issued sounds closer to the feminine gender. Alec Roytman was boisterous and good-humoured, his fist closed easily round a tankard of beer. His moustache was waxed jauntily at its ends; Max's drooped in anti-climax over his lips, while he drank nothing except pale lemon tea sucked through a lump of sugar. The two men stood oddly together. But a *landsmann* you had to help.

Alec took a hand in the destiny of Max and Rosa Litvinoff. It would not end with his marshalling them along the Antwerp quays for the correct embarkation point for Tilbury. While he showed Max the ropes his wife Rebecca nursed her young and compared pregnancies with Rosa. In 1913 the latter's first was due round about the Ninth of Ab, a solemn day in the Hebrew calendar recalling the destruction of the Temple, while Rebecca's third would be due two months later, during the Feast of Tabernacles, *Succoth*. The first date vaguely corresponded to some time in the second week of the Gregorian August, the second in the middle of October.

Older than Rosa by several years, Rebecca was plump and

experienced. 'You're carrying heavy', she informed Rosa. 'You will have a fine boy, please God.' She reassured Rosa. 'Stay with us. There'll be a person from the committee when we get off the boat in London. They look after you properly over there.' A portmanteau term, this 'committee', for any organisation caring for the dispirited Jewish nomad. 'Alec has a friend, another *landsmann*, who's finding us a room. He'll get one for you too.'

Sure enough, following a couple of nights in the Jews' Temporary Shelter beside the London docks (an entire diaspora had passed through those forbidding portals) they reached a haven at last, one room for the Roytmans, one for the Litvinoffs, in Christian Street (strange name, the only *goy* ever to pass that way was the postman), a stone's throw from the Whitechapel Road.

In the summer of 1913 Rosa's son duly arrived, as divined by Rebecca Roytman. Alec, a man of resource, had already acquired a bench in a courtyard in Bethnal Green, centre of the woodworking trade, to start on his road to affluence – he never got there – as a master table-maker. Max was directed to the Garment Workers Union, for it doubled as an unofficial employment exchange, where we have already encountered him making the acquaintance, through the good offices of a basting-hand, of Mr Cohen with the pebble glasses. Soon he too was earning a livelihood of sorts, piecework, wielding a seven pound flat iron.

Beyond this alien ethnic enclave, transplanted from the East European ghetto, with its card games, tea drinking and expensive baby photographs, and borrowing a sixpence here and there to tide you over the long week, another world was engaged in important business. This was the Triple Entente and naval rivalry and frontier conflicts that served to remind nations how much they distrusted each other. Not a great deal of this reached the columns of the *Zeit*, East London's local Yiddish newspaper price three-ha'pence and to be read from right to left. The *Zeit* concerned itself more with pogroms in Russia, Tilbury shipping intelligence and the latest melodrama that Kessler, the Jewish Henry Irving, was staging at the Pavilion theatre down the road. The assassination of an Archduke at Sarajevo warranted four lines at the bottom of the page. But perhaps this was because that tragic event had already made headlines in the English Press the week before – the *Zeit* had no vanity about being first with the news.

August 1914 might, indeed, have attracted small attention in Whitechapel were it not for the orders that suddenly came flooding into the tailoring workshops. A visit to Bloom's for a salt-beef nosh was now a more frequent occurrence, while Alec Roytman couldn't keep up with orders for his kitchen tables.

Outsiders now made a sprinkling of khaki among the crowds in Petticoat Lane. Jews commanding adequate English expanded their horizons in the newspaper room of the Whitechapel public library and studied the photographs in the *Jewish Chronicle* of native sons killed in action. The blotchy half-tone rectangles were soon filling entire pages, some of them depicting officers even, descended from Jews whose onion boat would have arrived at Tilbury not just years before, but decades ago. These had paid the price of elevation to the ranks of the true British. How tastefully the *Chronicle* laid them out, under the heading 'Made the Supreme Sacrifice'. And Gus Harris, the music hall comic, commemorated their heroism at the Paragon theatre (soon to become a cinema) in his song 'The Only Yiddisher Scotchman in the Irish Fusiliers'. Whitechapel in general was not unduly disturbed. Its denizens hardly thought of the outcome of the Great War – whoever won, it didn't relate to them. Weren't they life's perennial losers?

Rebecca Roytman now had three children, the last a girl. Her arrival prompted Alec to go in search of a dwelling rather more ample than the room sheltering them in Christian Street, and he found something suitable in Fuller Street Buildings, rent seven shillings a week, much closer to his Bethnal Green workshop. The Roytmans occupied door number eight (the term 'flat' was outside the residents' vocabulary) up three flights of stairs which grew cleaner as you mounted, because of the reducing traffic. The yard below, perhaps 15 feet square, housed three toilets and the communal dustbin, though as the tenement lacked a front door anyone could walk off the street, wait for a toilet to become unoccupied, and use it.

For the Litvinoffs it was as though a close relative had emigrated. Christian Street now lost its warmth. In any event Rosa was expecting again, so she spoke to her husband of their need for more space, a room with a kitchen. Max received the news in some surprise; it had not occurred to him. But with Pinny almost a year old Rosa heard of such accommodation in Redman's Road. She went down to the stables behind Gardiner's Corner (who, today, with the area a network of one-way 'race tracks', recalls that celebrated naval and military outfitter, 'Established 101 years'?) and her possessions were piled on to a horse and cart for the mile-long migration from Whitechapel to Stepney Green, at a charge of a shilling with twopence for a drink.

Rosa was what might be called a very definite person so, when told of the decision to move, Max performed the irrelevant act of nodding his approval. As a matter of fact, Redman's Road was located much more conveniently for his daily walk to Mr Cohen's, though it lengthened considerably his evening pilgrimage to Goide's café. However, Max was reconciled to the reality that you can't have everything, and when a Zeppelin dropped a bomb on Christian Street – to the amazement of the *goyim* who thought the Jews, as foreigners, had a secret arrangement with the Kaiser that spared them such horrors – he saw how sensible Rosa had been. Stepney Green was much safer than Whitechapel proper, which attracted many near-misses intended by the German raiders for the docks.

This brings us to our first encounter with Maksim Litvinoff on that day, so unlike any other, in September 1917, and his boarding of a number twenty-three bus, destination Russia. As the playwrights might put it, 'Exit, to the sound of distant alarums'.

Max had done his all for England by leaving behind three tiny British subjects tucked up in their beds, with another on the way. This fourth son was born roughly in the same week as Lenin uttered the historic cry 'All power to the Soviets!' – perhaps a few days later, maybe earlier. According to some stupid English law for which no parallel had existed in the old country, Rosa Litvinoff was required to report the child's arrival to a gentleman known as the Registrar of Births, Deaths and Marriages. It took her a week or two to get round to it, what with mothering four children under the age of five, and occasionally shepherding them to the nearest basement shelter. Then she had some difficulty finding the Registrar's office.

As to her new baby's date of birth, she knew it by the Julian calendar then still operative in Russia, and the Hebrew calendar, but in London everything was reckoned by the Gregorian. So the Registrar himself, while Rosa worked backward in time on her fingers, decided on a date, 23 November. He passed the certificate across his counter for the mother's signature. Another difficulty: Rosa could write her name where necessary in the Cyrillic alphabet, and in Hebrew, but had not as yet mastered the Latin characters. With a despairing sigh the Registrar placed his finger on the appropriate column and she signed with a cross. Underneath he wrote: 'The mark of Rosa Lietvenoff (as he spelled it), Mother, 45 Redman's road, E.1'. So much ambiguity, but one thing was beyond dispute: I was born.

Rosa must surely have thought about her husband Max often, recalling memories of her man with a tear as she retired to bed, listening for the postman's rat-tat and a message carried from Odessa across blood-soaked Europe. If so, she rarely spoke of him to her children. No letter arrived. Maksim Litvinoff, from being a father and a trousers-presser, took on the nature of an unspoken assumption. It could not be controverted, four children being proof positive.

Until her youngest arrived Rosa visited the bureau of a Russian Consular official each week to receive seventeen shillings and sixpence, constituting her allowance as a wife and half-a-crown for each of her children. Prime Minister

A Very British Subject

Kerensky, grateful or otherwise, was doing his duty. But with the simultaneous birth of the Bolshevik regime and her new son Barnet, that bureau ceased to exist. Russia was now classified a traitor by the Allies, practically an enemy, with its affairs handled by that other Maksim Litvinoff, the educated one, who was not so much an ambassador as a hostage. For the dependents of the men sent from Euston Station he had not a rouble. The British could look after them now. After all, didn't this capitalist society claim to be the greatest empire the world had ever known? From the greatest empire, it must be said, there came not a shilling.

Now the epilogue. This had to await another war, when all four sons of Rosa Litvinoff were themselves in khaki, the fourth married to Sylvia, fourth child of Alec and Rebecca Roytman.

2 • In the Buildings

As I write, Fuller Street Buildings, which remained stoutly perpendicular while it rained cats, dogs and Hitler's bombs, are no more. Fuller Street itself has all but disappeared – cut short, diverted and town-planned into a colony of respectable houses, each with a bathroom and individual toilet. Bethnal Green has lost all specific identity on the map, subsumed within an amorphous region bearing a name reminiscent of the Middle Ages, Tower Hamlets.

Bethnal Green, near the heart of a city that was the heart of a great empire, was so thickly populated it claimed two members in the House of Commons, Colonel Nathan for the north-east constituency, Sir Percy Harris for the south-west. I can still feel the squeeze of Sir Percy's large hand on my nine-year-old fingers as he presented me with my prize for coming sixth in the class examinations. It was a book titled *The Sights of London*, introducing me to such wonders as the Mansion House, Guildhall, the Monument and Hampton Court Palace. Of course, I already knew of the Tower of London and Buckingham Palace, so often mentioned at school as being about the most important buildings in the universe.

We had imposing structures closer to home: the red-bricked public wash-house, visited once a week for a warm all-over bath (children a penny, bringing their own soap and towel, in the second class), and the pubs, faced with green or yellow marble tiles and mostly dedicated to a nineteenth-century duke or princess. I preferred the name honouring the pub round the corner in Bacon Street beside the timber yard. It was called the 'Angel and Crown'. Little gentile girls guarding babies in prams waited outside while their parents sang beerily or performed a 'knees-up' within, particularly on Saturday nights. I assumed, not altogether correctly, that only Christians entered pubs, and this marked them as a people inferior to the Jews. If ever the Jews made merry, or shouted and brawled, it would happen among themselves, in private.

Graceful churches, stared at only when you needed to know the right time, formed other prominent landmarks of the district, beside more modest places of Christian worship converted into synagogues. These latter have since been adapted as mosques and Indian temples. We had banks too, though no one I personally knew until I was a grown man patronised a bank. I opened my first account with Barclays at Dalston Junction, remote from Fuller Street, at the age of 28 after the war, depositing my army gratuity of sixty pounds. The establishment now sports an Asian designation, for it funnels the proceeds of workshops whose sewing-machines hum beneath the charge of ladies in saris.

Sixty years ago this enclave in a corner of Bethnal Green constituted the whole of my world, bounded by Victoria Park to the north, the London and North Eastern Railway in the west, Whitechapel Road in the south, and unknown terrors leading to the enemy territory of Shoreditch further east. It would be so till I reached the age of 13 in 1931, when my family emigrated to the wilds of Hackney. Most Sundays would then find my brothers and me, severally or together, walking all the way back to Fuller Street and its environs, unable to acclimatise to a new roost. One could take the bus the length of Mare Street as far as the Salmon and Ball pub that marked the entrance to Bethnal Green Road, but that luxury required twopence for the fare.

Our buildings were twins, Numbers 54 and 56 Fuller Street, and affixed to each other Siamese fashion. We were domiciled at door three in Number 54. Never having once penetrated Number 56 I cannot speak of its backyard with open communal dustbin. This was of giant size in our yard, which also contained the three toilets, no locks, that the ten families shared. My mother once lost a ten-shilling note, accidentally thrown

In the Buildings

away with the rubbish. We all chased down below and she overturned the great bin, scattering its contents, while we helped her pick over each little heap. Mother ejaculated a low sound of triumph; she had found the note.

Tenants could take possession at Number 56 and move out again without impinging on our lives. At Number 54 a change of residency became a major event, so rarely did it occur. I can recall to this day the excitement when the Shermans at door six surrendered occupation to the Shapiros, and the morning Lily Shapiro left in a taxi to be married to a tall gentlemen's tailor she had met, it was related, at the La Bohème dance hall in the Mile End Road. The venue was much discussed in our part of the world. I took its glamour on trust, never having seen it.

Lily Shapiro's marriage I remember most vividly, because my mother and step-father Solly Levy quarrelled that very morning over the wedding present. They were in one of their non-speaking periods. She had left it to him, he affected oblivion. Mother threatened that without the present she would stay away, so Solly had rushed to his sisters round the corner in Hare Street, and after much spilling of handbags returned with the two guineas statutory if you were invited as a couple to the whole affair – reception, dinner and dance. You would die rather than give less. The publicity could prove fatal.

I was three years of age in 1921 when Alec Roytman the furniture-maker arrived at Redman's Road in Stepney to inform my mother Rosa that door three in the buildings where his family occupied the flat described as door eight, had fallen vacant and he had snapped up the two rooms and scullery behind the door on Rosa's behalf. Much of man's inner nature went unremarked in those times, and Alec's character, so far as anyone wished to know, was beyond reproach. To be sure, he acknowledged some responsibility towards Rosa, and not only because she was a handsome woman of 27 from the old country, tied to her fatherless four children. Alec recognised that he was in some measure instrumental in persuading Maksim Litvinoff to take the Euston train back to Russia during the war when Maksim, as others had done, might have adopted the 'kiss my arse' attitude to the British government's invitation to enlist either in London or their native land. Alec himself had safely returned, so loyalties demanded that he keep half an eye on Rosa and her brood.

She duly brought the children to Fuller Street, and the old association between the two families, initiated on the Antwerp quays, resumed. Rosa was not on the market, that was obvious, and Alec wasn't looking. That is, not deliberately. He liked a drink, and was a good friend. If his disposition led him into a certain coarseness of speech and action, that was the way in the furniture trade. Familiarity never crossed the border to monkey business. Alec's Rebecca had already produced five lusty children, tucked upstairs in their own flat.

For all ten families inhabiting our building, their two rooms commingled functions. Not much could be done about the scullery, already bursting with gas cooker, sink and washing copper, except to sit the children a few at a time at the table at meal times. Beds took up space in both main rooms, the one opening on to the landing being called the middle room, the other, facing the street, the front room. I had no idea that homes existed with a room entirely reserved for sleeping.

In our case an additional function was likewise spread over the two. Rosa paid the rent (seven shillings a week to start but increasing) and fed her family by making dresses. She had to accommodate her Singer machine, while her middle room table was usually covered with patterns and work in progress. The front room boasted a full-length mirror where customers tried on their garments for fitting at least twice before Rosa pronounced them finished and ready for ironing on the middle room table, then to be parcelled in brown paper and pins for taking away.

My three brothers and I learnt the types of fabrics among our earliest words – georgette, crêpe de Chine or taffeta for party frocks, serge and worsteds for afternoon dresses, silks (pure and artificial) for blouses; and the stylish colours – Florence Mills meant a light brown, royal blue was half way between light and dark, salmon pink to make the boys wink.

In the Buildings

Mother mainly worked alone, though in busier periods she took in Lily Shapiro from door six, besides Joanie the Polish Catholic 'printiss' who came at age fourteen like a ray of the brightest sunshine. Joanie remained, on and off, for some two years, well after Solly Levy entered the household in 1924 as Rosa's second husband, and Joanie was nursing babies as well as learning the trade. Thereupon she left. It took several years of schooling before I associated 'printiss' with the English word 'apprentice'.

Ethnicity obeys instinctive rules demonstrating how closely humankind resembles lower creature worlds. All the parents occupying Number 54 were immigrant Jewish, a species self-determined to breed among its own, though no authority had ordained it that way. The sole exception was the caretaker, who occupied the topmost flat on the fourth floor nearest to heaven. A male caretaker was a power like God, unseen and inaccessible. A woman holding the office, on the other hand, spent her life up and down the stairs, in and out of the flats. She could be relied upon to transmit gossip, in which we were all vitally interested, from door to door. Sixty years along memory's deceitful path can delude, but those ten families lie imprinted on my mind as indelibly as my name, to be borne throughout life. We formed a community of totally shared experience, as though predestined to do so from the moment in the Book of Genesis that Adam and Eve were expelled from the Garden of Eden.

Nowadays the term community suffers from nostalgic misuse, connoting all the virtues – kindness, mutual assistance, banishment of loneliness, joint endeavour and harmony. If only it were so! Our community in the buildings was torn by jealousies and disputes, garnished with selective snobbery and fragmented through contempt. That, and ignorance. Topping it all, a heavy incubus, lay the cynicism of the deprived. At the grocer's, where credit was never refused, we invariably passed a two-shilling piece across the counter monarch side up in the hope that it would be mistaken for half a crown. Helping hands certainly existed, though often spurned due to false pride. Immigrants without education who dropped by nature into Fuller Street stayed without education. Yiddish was their lingua franca and the *goyim* along the street belonged to a civilisation that you wanted no part of and despised.

In our community children were sent to school not because learning was considered important but because the system decreed so, as it said stealing was an offence and a respectable girl never walked out with a married man. Charles Booth's survey *London Life and Labour*, published in 1892 yet still valid in the 1920s (the First World War changed society hardly an iota), stigmatised this section of Bethnal Green as the most impoverished in the metropolis, drifting into crime. Our buildings sheltered an alien underclass into the bargain. However, unwilling elders were gradually led by their children along the road to awareness and adjustment. But the process was slow.

London harboured many other Jews, probably the majority, who worried for their families, brought home regular wages, treated their wives and children to outings and cared about schooling. Living in our buildings indicated that you knew few such people, and likely as not the man about the house, should he exist, was an absolute incompetent or light-headed buffoon, perhaps a gambler and probably a drinker into the bargain. We had a wife-beater (I employ a term not then in common currency) on the ground floor immediately beneath door three. Mr Portas the plumber differed from the rest of us in being, like my future stepfather, London born of Sephardic stock for whom Yiddish was a foreign language. Mrs Portas suffered bouts of delirium, and on occasion burst into continuous song till silenced by a hoarse throat. Within the plumber's household no water tap was fixed; they used the one in the back yard so we others were abreast of much of their domestic arrangements. Mr Portas would absent himself for days at a time, that we also knew, as screams from his wife usually heralded his periodic return. Their youngest, a boy at infant school with me, on one occasion suffered a mishap that resulted in soiled trousers. I remember remaining with him in his tearful discomfort when, to my surprise, his sister suddenly arrived with a

In the Buildings

fresh pair. This would not have been possible in our home, for my brothers and I possessed only one pair of trousers each. Mother had to find the time to run up a new pair on her machine from spare bits of fabric, to replace the unwearable by the unsaleable.

Never let it be said that we in the buildings were unhappy. Since no measure of wealth came into our ken we remained unaware of being actually poor. Street beggars singing for a coin we judged as poor, no less than the old ladies wrapped in rags underneath the railway arches linking Bethnal Green Road with Commercial Street. We passed the homeless women – one of them cradled a kitten – on our way to and from the Cambridge Picture Palace which we patronised half-price on matinées and stayed two programmes round. Sometimes we 'bunked' in without paying, through a side door leading to the gallery lavatory.

The Kollicks in door five directly above us were obviously poor, as revealed by the absence of linoleum on their floor, and because their Hymie, a massive untamed youth unemployed for the entire period of our acquaintance, idled his time away at the Bacon Street corner shabbily covered in an ancient overcoat through all seasons. Hymie occasionally pushed a barrow of timber deliveries for pennies. Demented Mrs Kollick entertained fantasies that one of the tramps coming off the street (no front doors to the buildings) and using our toilets might be her runaway husband.

Growing up in the buildings we four Litvinoff boys felt no intimation of envy or deprivation when we observed our playmates greeting a father's return from work, and a man bringing his son a tin drum or a scooter. Sammy across the landing in door four possessed a scooter, and their middle room boasted a piano. Sammy's unprepossessing father, a tailor's presser with a stoop, rarely looked awake. He held two jobs down, and with just two children their home appeared unoccupied. The ménage struck us in door three as most peculiar. Our mum turned her nose up at the parents. They were Polish Jews, and did not rate highly in the estimation of anyone born in Russia proper. I accepted their inferiority as a truism from about the age of five.

How was I to understand otherwise? We brothers never confided our deepest thoughts to each other, never asked mother to speak of our own dad, or her childhood in Odessa. We only picked up snatches of information from chance remarks passed in the course of a day involved with affairs of more immediate moment. Possibly, as the baby of the family, I was kept deliberately in the dark. More likely, we all preferred it that way. Mother might have revealed more had one of her children been a girl. The house was bereft of intimacies and such demonstrations of affection as a maternal kiss. Yet we all worshipped her.

Sleeping two to a bed and three to a bed when Solly came, and with him further babies in quick succession, there hardly occurred a second of privacy. We were not the only children in the street without an occasional gift or an annual birthday card, though one red letter day would never be forgotten. Brother Pinny, a year and a half my senior, won a real football in a competition.

We were important patrons of the cobbler, whose little shop we passed four times a day back and forth from school. Mr Bailey (for years I called him the 'shiester', not realising I was speaking Yiddish) encouraged business by placing a jam jar filled with tiny nails in his window. A customer had to guess the number of nails, and the nearest to the correct answer would win the prize – an authentic twelve-panelled leather ball enclosing an inflatable bladder as seen in picture books.

Our four pairs of boots frequently made the route to Bailey's. As he took them in he would ticket them, and on retrieval was handed, together with the money, our estimates of the contents of the jam jar on a scrap of paper. Excitement mounted. You always stopped at the window in Hare Street to scrutinise those nails, with some youngsters making calculations by a formula of their own devising. In our family it was taken for granted that one brother would not trespass on another's estimate.

In the Buildings

In due course Pinny's name appeared in the window. The good news spread as quickly as the result of the Oxford and Cambridge boat race. My brother, who was the quiet one of the four and a loner (we were all loners), walked down Fuller Street head held blissfully high, the local hero. How had he done it? Pinny was by no means noted for being particularly clever – not yet anyhow, though he was the first in the buildings to win a scholarship to Parmiter's, Bethnal Green's grammar school in Victoria Park, where I rapidly followed as the second. Pinny revelled in his newly-acquired popularity with the football but kept us in the dark.

Another jar of nails now occupied the place of honour in Bailey's window. Tension gathered afresh. A trail of youngsters brought their boots for repair. The cobbler could barely cope with the increased trade. We begged mother prematurely to allow our boots to go in so as to qualify for the next competition, although this entailed the wearing of plimsolls in all weathers pending their return. What Pinny could achieve was surely within the competence of the other three.

Rosa, however, put a stop to the fever. Mr Bailey had awarded the football to Pinny not because he had been closest to the count. He had no time for counts, Mr Bailey told mother. It had gone to a member of our family, any member, because we were such good customers, four pairs of boots every few weeks. Did she need to spoil a glorious occurrence with disillusionment so absolute? Its effect on us all was cruel. Rosa was bred a realist; magic had no place in her existence. Pinny's football nevertheless performed yeoman service down our street, and once was brought to the park for a real game, eleven a side. Alas, it failed to withstand the constant usage. Ere long we in Fuller Street were again reduced to a bundle of tightly packed newspaper tied with string to make a ball.

Retrospectively, mother's haughtiness regarding the upbringing of her children, which ostensibly kept the penury of the household a sacred secret, appears to have heaped unnecessary suffering upon us. Truly, conscious upbringing barely existed: each among us, in his own way, was a wild, untended plant in a garden of neglect. Yet charity, while not given readily, was available to the Jewish poor in the East End of London. However, she shrank from visiting the office of the Jewish Board of Guardians near Petticoat Lane to submit a claim for assistance. Winter overcoats were available there, scrounged from local manufacturers, but the Litvinoff boys possessed no overcoats. Our boots had little life in them well before they went into Bailey's, which was why Manny, the athletic and accident-prone second eldest, caught a fragment of rusty metal in his foot while playing leap-frog in the street. (The provision of boots on request at the Jewish Board of Guardians constitutes a gem of a short story in Manny's *Journey through a Small Planet*, published by Michael Joseph in the 1970s.)

The local Irish, fugitives from the Black and Tans, sought the intercession of the parish priest for such requirements, and made no bones about it. How could they, with the footware so easily recognisable, tipped with iron studs that responded bell-like with every step, and doubtless originating as army surplus? In the buildings the unwritten rules dictated that charity was shameful. You told juicy tales about a third party to your heart's content, but never exchanged personal confidences with a neighbour. Probably such stories circulated concerning the social and economic situation of Rosa and her sons, for one day she answered a knock on the door to be confronted by a well-dressed stranger from the orphanage.

It was a grim Victorian institution located at Norwood in South London and spoken of as a prison. The man explained otherwise. Norwood would give the children a better start, he promised. Hebrew instruction was included with a general education. Norwood was prepared to accept all four of us, we would join the Boys Brigade and other clubs, while sports would develop our physique. The man assured Rosa that on reaching the age of thirteen we would each receive *Barmitzvah* and be granted a celebration. Naturally, she could have us back for the holidays.

Rosa wanted none of it: the separation, the stigma, the

children's home-sickness! In reality, the Norwood Jewish orphanage was barely distinguishable from an English public school of the period, with the discipline of morning prayers, regular meals, encouragement of hobbies and, no doubt, the same bullying. On their departure the governors undertook to see its charges apprenticed in an honourable trade with a kind master-tailor or hairdresser. Two of those known to have passed through Norwood finished up in a Labour cabinet.

We continued to attend the local elementary school, suffering torments of deprivation when a penny or two might have enabled our participation in a class treat by bus to a concert at the People's Palace in Stepney, or a nature trip to Epping Forest. The Litvinoff boys took their humiliations as routine and sat dumb at their desks after the summer holidays while others, and this included Sammy from door four, told of their week by the sea at Southend or Margate. I first saw the sea when a boy scout of twelve, a memory that allows me to stake a connection with the old Duke of Wellington. The royal collection of pictures contains one by the German painter Winterhalter. It depicts the aged victor of Waterloo presenting a gift to the baby Prince Arthur, his godson. That child, as a crusty octogenarian Duke of Connaught, stood beside me during a visit to our scout camp at Worthing. I like to recall the occasion as my *Barmitzvah*.

Who owned the buildings? Interesting point. Property dealing has for centuries attracted Jews as a congenial avenue to affluence. Evidently the worse the slum the more profitable proved the transaction, both to vendor and buyer, particularly in the East End. Such housing schemes as the Guinness Trust and council accommodation merely skimmed the surface and were only available, deliberately or otherwise, to British citizens. Ownership of the Fuller Street buildings, for all we knew, changed during a respite from prayers in the synagogue, or at the turn of a card at a gaming table.

Monday was rent day. The landlord, accompanied by a prize-fighter type, collected personally. Sammy's mother next door referred to him as the 'rentlord', a reasonable enough solecism I suppose. But we were never aware of his exact identity. He took the money, entered the details in the rent book, scrawled a signature and passed on. He could have been anybody, possibly an impersonator. The occupiers would have been none the wiser.

Successive landlords not only acquired the property but inherited the arrears of rent, which tenants incurred as of right. I cannot recall a single eviction for non-payment. On the other hand, voluntary departures always took place early on Mondays, before the anticipated arrival of the man for his dues. Escape was meticulously planned, without leaving a forwarding address. Thus did Alec Roytman pack his burgeoning family (eight children ultimately) in a lorry in 1927 and make off, it transpired, for Holyhead and Dublin. We all knew of the operation but breathed not a sound.

Alec had not matured into a responsible husband and father. The family's removal to a distant atmosphere was only incidental to his personal flight. He acted to elude an inquisitive workshops inspector who suspected Alec of sticking used stamps on the insurance card of an employee and availing himself of the weekly deduction at his pub. Sadly, Alec tended to fritter away money on alcohol, a habit cultivated during his enforced wartime sojourn in the old country. Prior to their departure the Roytmans sold off the contents of their home within the buildings. Rosa bought their sofa, together with a chest of drawers that stood firm against a wall despite its lack of rear legs, a snip at 15 shillings.

The landlord lost nothing thereby. Controls being non-existent, a newcomer paid off the arrears of his predecessor through increased rent. Our class of tenant was provided with shelter, nothing more. Periodically, the district sanitary inspector would make his rounds to hear complaints: the entrance hall and staircase unlit at night; the stairs never cleaned; a damaged toilet awaiting rectification for weeks – all to little purpose. Residence in those buildings stamped us as Neanderthal survivors emerged from some remote desert or jungle, fortunate to join a civilised society. If it wasn't to our liking we could return to where we came from, and good riddance. Alternatively, the landlord may have paid the sanitary inspector off to leave him to scratch a living in peace.

Appealing to the gentile caretaker to repair a broken floorboard or plaster a hole so as to repel the annual summer invasion of the Red Army (the bed bugs' affectionate sobriquet) likewise proved fruitless. We enjoyed hilarious moments observing mother, oil can in hand, chase them back to base. What comprised the caretaker's functions we could not properly divine. He was a centurion simultaneously ridiculed and feared. A new one might demonstrate initial brave intention by actually disinfecting the toilets and hosing down the yard. Then, like an academic achieving tenure, he soon learned better ways. The male caretaker I remember best appeared truly a Neanderthal himself, dwarf-like and with a dog's bark of a speech defect. He spent most of his time on the roof among his pigeons. Alley cats left their traces in all corners of the stairs until their capture in her baskets by the lady from the RSPCA (my horror of cats persists to this day), while neighbourhood prostitutes entertained their clients in the dark.

For a female caretaker Mrs Murphy stood in a class alone. This lean and unkempt soul might well have materialised out of an early Punch cartoon meriting a caption of the 'charlady with bottle' category, so rarely was she completely sober. On occasion she would be seen with a strapping fellow, whom we surmised to be her husband, for there existed two streetwise ragamuffin children with an alarming vocabulary in obscenities. Mrs Murphy discovered an original method of supplementing her income, such as it was, via the Blundell's tallyman. The old-established store in City Road flourished on the weekly payments system resorted to by many working-class families, ours included. The tallyman's practice was to press further goods – curtains, towels, linoleum – on customers before clearance of the debt from a previous purchase. Thus you would likely be in hock to Blundell's for perpetuity. Mrs Murphy treated the tallyman as the horn of plenty. She took anything and everything, retaining nothing. Instead, she hawked the goods cut price from door to door in the buildings for cash in hand. Was ever retribution visited upon Mrs Murphy? We never knew. However, God surely moved in a mysterious way in the buildings, for subsequently our stepfather Solly acquired a two-valve radio on the 'never-never'. Unemployment caused him to fall behind with his payments and the radio was promptly repossessed.

When Solly came to live with us we had not been apprised of a marriage ceremony; nor did we ask. As far as I understood, all daddies appeared in a family ready-made as he did, to be found sleeping at home in the morning as though taken in like a stray animal for a pet. We already knew him, of course, as an habitué of the card evenings regularly held at the Roytmans, where mother used to join the wives for lemon tea and a chat. If asked, Solly would roll up a shirt sleeve and display the tattoo on his arm. They were a rough-hewn lot, Alec's friends, all immigrant furniture-makers except for Solly, who was a handsome young English Jew with a passion for cards that overcame the alien ambience and its language.

Solly had served in the Royal Fusiliers, rising to sergeant, and was gassed in the trenches of the Somme. He always carried a photograph of himself astride a camel at the Pyramids, and during the interval between war's end and his arrival in Fuller Street had sought his fortune in South Africa. He must surely have been the only Jew to have failed on the Rand, for he returned to an East End tailoring workshop where he sewed the sleeves into men's coats at the usual piecework rates. Mother looked well as an independent widow, taller than average, her mane of dark hair gracefully held back in a bun at the nape of her neck, and with her own little business. She rarely had a kind word for his unmarried sisters in Hare Street. They on their part did not conceal a conviction that Solly had been entrapped.

As for his character, it was less apparent than his charm – soft voice, sprightly gait, toothbrush moustache and light wavy thatch. He slipped imperceptibly into door three without

In the Buildings

exerting any fundamental change on our existence. He did not legally adopt us. In fact he hardly noticed us. Soon, to the delight of the brothers, a baby sister appeared. Mother gave her a smart Russian name then rare in England, Sonya. Proudly we pushed her pram up and down the street and to the park, shaking a rattle in her smiling face.

Not long afterwards mother gave birth again, to a boy for whom Solly demanded the very English name Gerald. We insisted on calling him Jackie. He was produced in January 1926, in our front room like Sonya, with Mrs Shapiro of door six assisting the midwife. Meanwhile, relations between husband and wife were not proceeding as harmoniously as might appear to be the case. Even as the population in the two-roomed flat increased, mother continued at her dressmaking, the four older boys relegated to lower priority. She had no alternative. The General Strike of 1926 and the ensuing slump put Solly out of work for weeks, tailoring being a seasonal occupation at the best of times. As a British-born citizen, and young enough, he might have tried his hand at a different occupation, but Solly was immovable from his groove.

The new husband spent a great deal of time in Hare Street with his hard-working mother and sisters, returning only to eat and sleep. His own father, with a grubby choker round his neck and reeking of beer, for which he was sent to Coventry by his family, knew no skilled trade. Solly might well have succeeded in life, for he was a great reader. He took George Lansbury's *Daily Herald* and borrowed library books too, mostly about the war, although his favourite read was *Penguin Island* by Anatole France. A regular customer for *Amazing Stories*, the American science fiction magazine available second-hand on purchase or exchange from a Bacon Street newsagent, Solly would hide behind its pages deaf to the crying of the children or the moan of the sewing-machine. For the rest, he allowed the world to revolve without his assistance, not once suggesting that we might seek a roomier abode. Except for childish me, he rarely spoke to the growing brothers save to send them out for the cigarette papers into which he rolled his Golden Virginia. Mother would raise her voice in anger at his failings as a provider. He had a stock reply: 'Do you want me to go thieving for you?' Still, shortly after Gerald's first birthday, another baby, David, arrived.

At this stage of our domestic expansion I had reached the age of embarrassed awareness, realising something was wrong. Families had no need for so many children. Where were we to put them all? I expect my brothers felt likewise, though the implication that parental intimacies alternated with the strife could not be articulated among us. We were four intensely private juvenile personalities now, incapable of releasing our emotions. The street filled the gap. Neighbouring boys with whom we took our leisure forewarned us. "Ere', one of them once smirked at me, 'your mum's goin' to have another one.'

'No, she's not!' I protested, despairingly. Surely it was all over and done with, the shifting around of sleeping accommodation, the summoning of Mrs Shapiro at night, the appearance of the mysterious lady described as the midwife! Not at all. Baby Frank duly appeared and we were eight, equally divided between two fathers. At this rate we would soon be running out of names. Pinny and I already attended grammar school, returning daily loaded with homework, but without an empty corner in which to discharge it.

Abie, the eldest among us and at 14 a reluctant beginner in the tailoring world, was bringing home ten shillings every week. He surrendered three quarters of his earnings for bed and board, but otherwise practised withdrawal. Manny, deprived to his distress of Parmiter's School (he achieved a near miss for the scholarship and could be admitted only for the 'reduced fee' of one pound each term, an insuperable condition), dropped, by osmosis, into a furrier's workshop. Solly continued as if none of this was his concern. To do him justice, he attempted with occasional gestures to bridge our hostility, but stepsons in quantity inevitably equate to a conspiracy of sullen silence.

We were gradually being turned into Englishmen of a

particular genus, the process having started in the elementary school beside St Matthew's in Church Row, a five minute walk from Fuller Street. The teachers there wrestled bravely or sarcastically with the East European names, according to their individual attitudes to the infiltration of their society by the alien hordes. In my class Mr Jones called an attendance register of 40 pupils each morning beginning with Aronowitz and terminating in Zelikovsky, all done so casually the names might have testified to a lineage sprung from the Normans accompanying William's invasion of 1066. Mr Parker, on the other hand, got the class sniggering with his insistence on describing two of us as 'Old tin potsky' and 'Old tin cansky'.

Schooling was a serious affair, harsh but thorough, with the cane in regular employ. Mr Jones bequeathed a heritage upon us with all the grace of a corporal drilling a platoon of conscripts. 'This is one of Shakespeare's sonnets', he informed us. 'Learn it by heart, or else . . .' We learnt it. Confuse Crécy with Agincourt and a lump of chalk hurtled across the room to sting your ear. Naming five countries within the British Empire, with the penalty for failure of writing them out 50 times, was easy: we owned one-fifth of the world's surface, including a few countries like Egypt coloured pink for good measure on the map in defiance of strict accuracy.

Before our family organised its moonlight flit (dawn, actually) from Fuller Street buildings and I had graduated to my new posh school, I could decline any noun of Latin's vast third declension while ascending the stairs two at a time. Yet until reaching my twentieth birthday I had not consciously spoken to anyone, except schoolteachers and doctors, with a university degree.

An epoch draws to its surreal close. One summer day in 1931 mother, her mouth full of pins, was on her knees adjusting the length of a special occasion frock in black lace guipure for an influential customer with contacts in the wide beyond. Observing the absence of Rosa's usual agility – yes, little Frank was not a year old but she was carrying again – the lady, somewhat dubiously, spoke of a vacant flat, owned by her friend Mrs Goldfarb behind a tobacconist's shop in Hackney. However, it was hardly possible that Mrs Goldfarb would take in a family with so many children.

Mother's response leapt from the tip of her tongue. 'You can tell her I have only four. The big ones are no longer children. Two of them go to work.' Abie was now sixteen. One week later Solly learnt about it for the first time, while mother was already packing. She had been accepted on the basis of four, with another child on the way.

We arrived in two stages, she with her husband and the young ones during the day, the big four by bus after dark. Mrs Goldfarb, discovering she had been deceived, gave vent to the most righteous indignation. In fact the accommodation was virtually uninhabitable, the ground floor being bare upturned soil awaiting new drain-pipes. However, we now boasted four rooms, our own front door and electric light. Pinny and I slept contentedly together on the 'parlour' floor. Six weeks and another baby son later, our bed arrived from Blundell's.

Miraculously, we grew up sane (well, relatively) and healthy, all nine children, sound enough a decade later to serve, Sonya included, in the struggle to make their country safe for democracy, hypocrisy and mediocrity. Baby Philip, the last, was compelled to linger impatiently in a dusty workshop until 1950 before donning Air Force blue.

I was recently lured to Bethnal Green Road again, and walked its length in quest of some relic to assure me that I had not dreamed it all. Every little store was now guarded by strangers from the Orient, while the junior section of our old library, which introduced me to Jules Verne and Wodehouse's tales of public school cricket and the antics of Psmith, had been usurped by their offspring, as eager for knowledge as ever we were. Surely this could not have been my ghetto? Then, gratefully, a familiar sight: Attenborough the pawnbroker, proclaiming his function with those same three brass balls of 60 years ago. This totem from that bygone age was proof enough. Mother would lodge her wedding ring there on Saturday

In the Buildings

mornings whenever, the evening before, Solly surrendered his week's wages at the greyhound track. Dear Attenborough! A memento of my two inheritances, Stonehenge and the Wailing Wall combined.

3 • Linsi

She would sometimes twist her way through the swirling traffic on the Place de la Concorde, would Linsi, and with an orgastic Oah! hug the ornate lamp posts, leaving me slightly but enviously bewildered. This was during the trembling year of the quietus, 1939, after Munich and before the Second World War. I too had succumbed to the city's spell. The sight of Notre Dame outlined from the Pont des Arts could bring me to the bridge at dawn. I used to stroll about the Latin Quarter with a weary fondness, notorious for taking a seat at the Capoulade until the waiter hove in view when, reluctant to yield up two francs for a table-served coffee, I fled.

But never could I bring myself to exhibit a passion for those lamp posts, certainly not in daytime. I suppose it was because Linsi was a poet, the only one I knew personally outside the contributors to my school magazine. Until Munich I had worked as a junior clerk in our local gas company building in Mare Street, Hackney. Now, in Paris, I informed people I was a writer. They believed me as I believed them. So far I had published nothing, and neither had they. The aspiration sufficed for appropriation of the label.

When I revealed to my mother that I was going to Paris to become a writer – they were my very words – she reacted as though I had taken leave of my adolescent senses. In the 1930s nobody, but nobody, voluntarily surrendered a job; and I was the first in our entire family to matriculate, the first to find employment that gave 52 pay days every year with two weeks of them as holiday, the first to escape a garment workshop. You didn't throw such promise back into a generous company's teeth. To reach so far as an initial interview I had artfully anglicised my ponderous Russian name. I was also the only one of us never to have reported at the employment exchange for the weekly dole. Now I would be like all my brothers, my mother prophesied tearfully, in and out of jobs for the rest of my life. Wishing to be a writer could not be accepted as a serious statement.

Yet here I was, in Paris, with a poet for a dear friend. We had met at what was called the Foyer Israélite in the rue de Vaugirard, a restaurant for poor Jewish students. A meal cost three francs 75 centimes for the full menu, two and a half francs for one plate only, but always with *pain à discretion*. This I took as a privilege, for not only was I a pretend-writer, I did not officially qualify as a student, merely a schoolboy turned junior clerk in rebellion. Linsi was sharing a table with her friend Sophie, years her junior and very sure of herself. Sophie was taking a degree in mathematics at the Sorbonne, where I used to attend public lectures on any subject taking my fancy.

One spoke in those days of 'interesting' people. Sophie was not interesting – had no need to be, since she was young and pretty, with parents living in Paris. Her father was a former Soviet vice-commissar. Linsi warranted the description 'interesting'. Times may have radically changed, but in that epoch an Englishman fraternising with the Central European refugees in Paris featured as a rarity. Many had not so much as seen an impecunious Englishman. In fact they knew hardly anyone unable to speak Polish or Czech or German. So Linsi took me up on the basis of my being an Englishman and a struggling writer. She picked me, I subsequently realised, in order to practise her English and establish a link, tenuous as it was, with the free realm of letters that began on the Anglo-Saxon side of the Channel. As far as Linsi was concerned, France could not be counted among the free. Foreigners lived there on sufferance, regularly hauled in by the police and required to show their papers. The police hardly bothered with the British, who were a privileged category in Paris.

Occasionally Linsi complained vehemently about her anonymity and neglect. 'No one will ever hear of me', she said.

'To become famous in France you must be English, or maybe Russian. The English have an important passport. The Russians come from a faraway, romantic country.'

I reddened guiltily, as did Sophie, though Linsi's eyes belied her cross remarks. As it happened, it was flattering to me to be allowed into her world, with its frustrations mingled with hope, and the fact that she so obviously came from what was then termed a 'good family' in some obscure corner of Central Europe. Three years in the London gas company had done little for my progress up the social scale.

She affected anger over matters that did not really annoy her, in the belief, I suspected, that this produced an impression of strength of character. She would lament at being so much older than either Sophie or me. Linsi confessed to 32, but then tangled up the decades in the stories she related of her past adventures and passions. It thrilled me to hear them because she granted confirmation that this really was *la vie parisienne*, and here I stood, an accepted part of it.

She pranced and gesticulated through the Latin Quarter, speaking in an excited falsetto, a woman trying to remain a girl. Yet now, as I recall, her eyes, brown and glaring bright, were physically all that remained of her youth. Privately I regarded her as old – in my calculation of the years how else? Her gait gave evidence to a pitiable frailty. When we walked along the Champs-Élysées (she loved the fairground beyond the Étoile) she needed to rest frequently and catch her breath. Sometimes we took the Métro. Not once, during my residence, did I indulge myself the luxury of those cheap Parisian taxis.

And the first time I heard Linsi speak in English! My temptation was to laugh out loud, though goodness knows my mother spoke the language no better. Linsi's accent was unlike any I had hitherto encountered in this city, home of a hundred accents. Her idiom, remarkable and fearless, almost volatile, included quaint borrowings from the classics no uncertain linguist would attempt.

'Puttees', 'bye-bye old chap', 'so flipperty-gibbet', all appeared to insinuate themselves into her style like uninvited guests for whom there was no appointed place at a feast. Blithely stumbling through the complicated syntax, she demanded my views on Anglo-American literature. What did I think of Kipling, Wilde, Theodore Dreiser? Did I prefer Katherine Mansfield to Mary Webb? The questions made me miserable. I had no idea people actually read those authors, except perhaps as books set for an exam. These Germans and their erudition! But she was not German, nor even Viennese. Linsi challenged me to pick her point of origin on the map of Europe, which was then undergoing violent redistribution. She ridiculed my guesses in peals of derisive laughter.

'You English are always so generous with other people's nationalities', she cried, 'and I'm still a mystery in the international jig-saw puzzle. Why don't you place me in the Heebrydes, with Mendelssohn? Hebrews should come from the Heebrydes.' At a record library on the Boulevard Saint-Michel (the original discothèque) they charged one franc to put the music on for you in a sound-proof cubicle. She had just emerged from listening to Fingal's Cave.

God had not been sparing with his gifts, Linsi related later. Among her many attributes, like walking and talking and writing poetry and doing impersonations, she possessed no less than three nationalities. This generous seasoning of frontier promiscuity rendered the simplest issues complex. What, for example, would she describe as her mother tongue? It was a puzzle. Tucked away there lay more political history than dates in an encyclopaedia.

Linsi first enriched an unappreciative family with her presence some time during the staid interregnum beginning with the dismissal of Bismarck and ending with a pop at Sarajevo. It was in a townlet in silly old Moravia, her birth certificate being decorated with the crest of the Austrian emperor. Her father, she said with a dismissive pout of her nearly bloodless lips, wore the turn-out of a prosperous central European lawyer. 'He emphatically disliked me', Linsi disclosed, 'because a girl becomes a woman and they were all such an' – she sought a word – 'interference.' When war came

A Very British Subject

he travelled regularly to Vienna, where he made speeches to the poor synagogue Jews.

Strange, it seemed to me. Weren't all Jews synagogue Jews? She brushed me off. 'I don't know, they were poor any old how. Father spoke to them of the integrity of Germany and the Habsburg Empire, saying that God would be punishing England. He had no time at all for the problems in his own home – such as, for instance, that his wife was growing crazy from her neuralgia.'

Affairs began to go awry with Linsi's father. 'His visits to Vienna grew not so frequent. He replaced them by excursions to Prague – never go to Prague, it will freeze your insides with its messy language. We always spoke German. I don't remember all the details, but he brought back some ideas concerning national rights and culture and those things. I never listened to him.'

However she told the garbled story, always differently, the declaration of peace found the lawyer on the right side. The family moved to Ostrava (she called it Ostrau), Moravia's capital. Linsi carried her altered nationality like a new hat. She became a Czechoslovak. 'Father liked the idea, though mother knew of nothing except her neuralgia. President Masaryk, you know, thought he had created a paradise for all the minorities. It didn't do very much for ugly schoolgirls like me.'

The reality of the situation must in truth have perplexed so upright a lawyer as Linsi's father. Had he been asked which minority he belonged to, it is doubtful whether he could have supplied a straight answer. The family obviously shared little in common with the Moravians. It could not be classed as Czech, or Slovak, or Polish, nor any of those other provincial types crowding into Ostrau, such as Magyars and Ukrainians. The father probably thought of himself as German, though not according to the Germans themselves. In any case who would happily lump himself with the vanquished?

Czechoslovakia took on the aspect of a zoo filled with every species of noisy animal, one which belonged to all of them while actually being part of none. This had to be fundamental to the Jews' situation in all the ages preceding the Second World War. Linsi would caricature for my benefit – Sophie had heard and suffered it all frequently before – her abortive ventures into patriotism. She had attended an uppish private school, a ridiculous ribbon in her stringy hair, and darted from group to group in a desperate effort to belong somewhere. Some spoke dialects she couldn't understand. Others left her waiting self-consciously outside their separate churches. The Jews of Ostrau were divided too, vertically and horizontally, in their various sub-denominations.

'It was confusion comprehended', she said, meaning 'confounded'. The beautiful girls had no such problem. They always found a boy to hold their books. In Paris Linsi had solved the conundrum, to her own satisfaction at least. She described herself as a Communist internationalist and intended, one day, to read Karl Marx. Well, she announced, one has to be *something*.

We were lingering on the steps of the Sorbonne when she informed me of one child, daughter of a German officer, who disdained from joining any of the squealing chauvinist groups. This girl was responsible for giving her the best advice anyone ever received. In her schooldays Linsi was not Linsi, but Leah, and the German girl whispered that its association with an Old Testament heroine revealed none too ancient a root in the Bohemian hills. She really must modify Leah to a name more appropriate to the land of her birth.

They had discussed the matter at length and Linsi was decided upon. The name pleased them, and the other, restricting her satisfaction to undemonstrative proportions, solemnly christened the lawyer's daughter with a light kiss on her forehead. The new Linsi, less reticent, proclaimed her delight to the skies and scrawled the name of her only friend over her exercise books. (Years later Linsi read in the *Pariser Tageszeitung*, which kept tabs on the wandering exiles, of the German officer's suicide; and of his daughter, apparently as composed as on that day in Ostrau, drowning herself in the Danube on the outskirts of Budapest.) By then so much had transpired for Linsi in her turn that the news affected her no more than an account of an art exhibition opened by President Lebrun.

The lawyer was diligently building his reputation as one of the leading citizens of Ostrau. He attended dinners and opened bazaars as often as the mayor himself. He subscribed to the Jews' soup kitchen and agitated for a lavatory in every home. In charity he practised no discrimination, for God loves those who love the needy. Thomas Masaryk had similarly started life in an insignificant byway of Moravia, and risen to the peaks of exaltation.

It was understandable perhaps that a man so attentive to tasks of benefit to all humankind as Linsi's father should overlook the stresses in his own family. Blind to the agonies suffered by his wife, the lawyer was also deaf to the morbid pleadings of his daughter. Linsi was approaching a skinny twenty and restless into the bargain. She was suffocating in a lifeless town that bore the character of observing Lent the entire year round. Where, in this confined space (half an hour's walk into the country and you faced a Polish sentry's rifle), would she find the opportunities to fulfil herself? 'You see', she confided needlessly, 'I was wondering about a husband.'

Situations such as these are frequently solved by the intervention of the fates, all working simultaneously. Destiny visited each member of the lawyer's family after a busy morning's litigation over the ownership of a cowshed. He arrived home to find his wife had been taken to a mental institution, never to emerge; his son had been refused a degree because the university authorities had deemed his thesis anarchistic; and from his daughter he was rewarded with a red-eyed defiant glare and a declaration that henceforth she intended to search elsewhere for recognition as a writer and rekindle her hopes for matrimony.

I was ill-prepared for the details when she retailed the vagaries of her love life, not realising at the time that for a refugee harassed from one frontier to the next there could be no tone of respectability that would not echo a hollow note. In any case, I issued from a society where sex had not yet broken the sound barrier. 'I had three lovers. One became my husband of the left hand. He was a kind man but a pervert – you know, always with the mouth.' I didn't know, being an innocent still of 21 in 1939. However, I listened in silent awe. 'The next one stole my money and went to Palestine to build the Jewish land. The third – I don't want to talk about him.'

'He was unkind?'

'Not at all! He's here in Paris, working at the Russian library.' Then she whispered: 'Sophie's father. She doesn't know.'

Clearly then, no husband. She had selected Berlin as her territory for conquest, deliberately eschewing Vienna, whose easy atmosphere should have made it an obvious choice. But Vienna was tarnished with family associations, and so Linsi determined on chillier climes to escape her vicious bourgeois circle. With what she ever afterwards considered calculated forethought, she begged one last favour of her father before the final goodbyes. She must visit a nose doctor and have that troublesome feature reconstructed into a more becoming shape.

The demand shocked the old man somewhat. Even were he blessed with imagination enough to recognise that a woman might desire to start a fresh life with the disadvantages weighing as lightly as possible against her, the implication that the family visage could be susceptible to improvement was distasteful. Hadn't he worn it contentedly these three score years? Nevertheless, he gave his consent and Linsi gravely underwent her transformation into a beautiful woman.

Not having known her in the Ostrau days but visualising her face as I do, I feel that the operation must be considered a failure. A light scar stretching from one nostril to the bridge of her nose bore witness to her efforts to secure cosmetic equality with the rest of her sex. Before that, she said, her face was like a gargoyle's. 'You know, like the gargoyles on Notre Dame.' A postcard of one of them was pinned up in her room off the Place de l'Odéon.

The shape of Linsi's face was parent to many of her thoughts. Her earliest stories told of insolent fairies with sour expressions, and of witches tying people in knots. In Berlin she performed in the cheaper cafés personalising the human clichés: an incipient poet apostrophising against a strong breeze while a puppy watered his trouser-leg; a top-hatted worthy (undoubtedly her father) hurrying through an after-dinner speech before his notes were completely consumed by the flame of an adjacent candle.

Burlesque was her forte. A thin volume of poetry, published in Berlin, bore the Freudian title *My Bestiary*. She spoke nostalgically of her years in the Prussian capital, where she had released herself in a tantalising prospect of the professional acclaim she yearned. Linsi's animal tales for children invariably included a professor of zoology (daddy again?) to inform the creatures they were impossible, because obviously animals don't speak. The bitterness haunting her imagination as she wrested humour out of any staid situation made her ripe for the Weimar Republic. Had the unknown Isherwood encountered Linsi before he changed trains, to transpose another ingredient into his Sally Bowles?

While this puckered imp wove her dreams in a half light of jests and tears, another greater gargoyle lurked in the darkness beyond, preparing his entry. Linsi struggled forward, one more heroic actor in that democratic Weimar farce entrusted with the hopeless task of saving a waning play. But there was not space enough for two devils in Berlin. Unobtrusively the iridescent little devil vacated the stage for this other one with the blinding gleam.

Trente-trois. Paris has benchmarked its turbulent epochs – 1789, 1870, 1940 – so 1933 barely warrants a memory there. Not so among those in whom I found company. All time was measured by its distance from *trente-trois*. The numeral cropped up in virtually every Jewish conversation. They were drenched by it, the occasion of Hitler's accession to power being the year of their flood. He had washed away the ground from under their feet and they were still seeking another soil.

First Germany ceased to be a homeland, then Austria, then Czechoslovakia. By the time I arrived in Paris the refugees constituted the most easily identifiable element of its population.

Moody, restless, unoccupied, all had grudgingly been accorded temporary sojourn in France provided they sought no employment while awaiting a visa for some distant shore. No country would readily receive them, and after years of studied acclimatisation to this alien way of life they still found themselves an indigestible colony in the cosmopolis of Paris. Britons and Americans, of course, like the ebony-skinned newcomers from the Ivory Coast, might all feel at home here, as did the Indo-Chinese, pert and unself-conscious as any *garçon* working the Latin Quarter bars. But the tense strangers from across the Rhine won few friends except as they themselves were, for they enjoyed no atmosphere save their own. Ernst Toller and Heinrich Mann remained their intellectual meat. On scrutinising the *affiches* on those circular street displays, the names they read – Aragon, Gide, Malraux – conveyed nothing.

When I first encountered Linsi she had already resigned from that crazy colony of bewildered Central European exiles. In contrast to them, she was as refreshing as the fountains at a meeting of the boulevards on a sweltering day. She loved to speak German, the natural music of her mind, while they avoided their own language to stutter in English or a travesty of French. They mostly spoke of New York and the day they would become United States citizens. She was the passionate wooer of Paris. They brooded in the cafés, peering furtively at the woman sipping at the next table but one, while she preferred to skim her palms along the walls of the Street of the Fishing Cat, or bang her overflowing spirit onto her tinny typewriter oblivious that full stops and capitals had been invented.

I feared for her vulnerability and innocence as she slept long, fretful hours to elude meal times, hoping to renew the strength that only food could bring. Few read her poems, let alone bought them, save the private public of her own tiny circle. She had a selection published at 15 francs on rough paper, bound cheaply in black, like an auctioneer's catalogue. (On the day I fled Paris, a privileged passport-holder escaping to London from the intimations of war, hundreds of copies lay scattered beneath her bed. I often wondered subsequently whether a different German read them; cheap entertainment lay there for a Gestapo agent with a literary kink.)

One evening remains with me. Sapped of all energy, she stretched motionless on her bed. Perhaps she had been typing the day away, to add another pile to the careless mountain on her table; or possibly on an errand to renew her visa at the Préfecture, the most hated building in the city; or to visit Notre Dame, the most adored. A nightgown hung loosely about her, ill-concealing her thin shoulders and breasts. She appeared so tired, as one expecting to die. I could not suppress the thought that she had not long to live, and little to live for.

'Tell me something, *mein nett Englander*', she murmured. Truly, I had so little to tell, from my experience. I was only beginning to grow up. So I told of what occupied me at the time, a book I was struggling to write and would never complete.

'You have so much strength, to write and write. Soon I will be dead and then you will not be too snobbish to make a book of me?' Even that terror she clothed in a phrase of comedy. 'The English love their poets most when they starve and die young.'

'You are too old to die young.' She laughed happily, the commonplace idea sounding novel for having been voiced in an alien tongue. I saw her once more, together with Sophie, at the Rothschild charity hospital.

With the war two months old and myself awaiting call-up, there arrived through the post that Notre Dame gargoyle postcard I had seen at her lodging. It said: 'Are you still alife?' My own aspirations were in disarray and, as my mother predicted, I had joined the unemployment queue. Nevertheless, I obtained the sanction then required from officialdom to export a sum of money, granted for relief of distress. So I sent Linsi a postal order for five shillings. Ludicrous as it seems now, and minute as it then was, I knew it could translate into a few lunches at the Foyer Israélite in the rue de Vaugirard. After this, silence.

Europe exploded. I tried to visualise Linsi, perhaps browsing through the open shelves of Gibert Jeune's bookshop in the Boulevard Saint-Michel. Sophie gave me no anxieties. Her strong legs and cool reasoning would see her through. Even in France Sophie was not a refugee for long. But did Linsi survive the German occupation, the deportations, the famine? Or was it her ghost alone that haunted the weeping streets of the Latin Quarter?

Twenty years passed. She had dropped from my preoccupations, almost from my memory, when I heard Linsi's voice again, in a letter from Montreal. She had seen a book of mine. What was I doing? Did I remember Paris? In my reply I enclosed that postcard from her room, surely evidence enough of time-tried fidelity, as well as a story published long before in one of the little magazines proliferating in the 1940s. It was based affectionately upon Linsi, and I anticipated a reply in like mood. Instead, there arrived a tirade. What had I turned into print but a horrible calumny, a portrait of some grotesque character that made her ill! As for the postcard, was that a cruel joke? Is that how she appeared to me, a gargoyle? In a few days another missive came, then a third, and a fourth, all dripping with such invective as to indicate a mind in disequilibrium. More letters followed, some in German, though I never wrote again. I dreaded every postal delivery.

She had survived the war, though as one of its casualties. Linsi had lived through the Nazi occupation of Europe, and for this I had prayed. However, she sent my thoughts racing to the many refugees I once detachedly observed in Paris. Some had surely died abruptly, by extermination. Others continued to inhabit a mental Auschwitz. One way or another, the curse of statelessness condemned them all.

4 • Dunkirk on my Mind

Anxious murmurings, bearing only indirectly on the crisis in Anglo-German relations, permeated the Hackney Employment Exchange in East London during the last days of August 1939. But why? The Anglo-German crisis had been played out after a fashion one year earlier, with its dénouement at Munich. It could not generate the same degree of tension in Hackney the second time round.

What concerned the members of the unemployed queue this morning related to a hitherto inconceivable phenomenon: work was available to all. Usually we signed our names on Monday and drew our dole money on Thursday, methodically, silently, without a hitch. The jobs suddenly on offer consisted of unskilled activity in the London parks: digging them up, wheeling the earth away, shifting bags of cement, all to do with the speedy erection of air-raid shelters. Hence the anxieties.

The work was not exactly on offer, in the precise meaning of the term. Refusal to accept entailed forfeiture of your weekly allowance, so it was virtually conscription. And many of those standing in line were appalled. We constituted a fraternity, and proffered liberal counsel to each other on ways to elude the pick and shovel brigade without incurring the dreaded stamp (like a death sentence) on one's card. It would record: 'Disqualified through refusal to accept employment', and be endorsed with the signature of a man in a striped city-suit.

'You can get out out of that kind of work', a companion in the queue informed me helpfully. 'All you need is a doctor's certificate. Chronic bad back or something.'

However, refusal never entered my head. This is the reason

why, on the morning of 3 September, I was not among the millions to hear Neville Chamberlain on the radio announcing to the nation that a state of war existed between my country and Germany. It was a Sunday, and I was digging up the soil for extra, overtime pay.

Navvying earned good wages, even for an unskilled labourer in tortoise-shell glasses that slipped down his nose each time he wielded his shovel. At 21, I spent the evenings writing my masterpiece, of which the most difficult part was holding a pencil in a calloused hand. My fellow-workers included some hardened career navvies, for whom this humble branch of the construction industry, war or no war, could be described as a piece of cake. Naturally, I decided that they belonged to England's great, unthinking lumpen-proletariat. How wrong! One of them casually replied to a foolish disclosure on my part of an intention to pursue a different, more elevated life style once the war was over. The man, fortyish and brawny, was shovelling muck into a wheelbarrow when he looked up to observe: 'That's why your people will never make a nation. You all want to be the guv'nor.' Fifty years on, the world has much changed. An independent state of Israel exists in the Middle East. Yet I still wonder if that navvy was altogether wrong.

Soon I became fairly skilled with the tools and ceased to disgrace myself. Nevertheless, when my call-up papers arrived I departed for Aldershot with rather more than relief. Soldiering would grant my ambition to produce the great war novel, as had Edmund Blunden from his experiences in the previous conflict with Germany. By the end of it all five chapters of the novel were written and one of autobiography – the one, needless to add, largely recycled from the other.

Before donning khaki I had borne the strongly visible traces, as I thought, of my Jewish ghetto origins. My parents had been immigrants. No doubt, by the standards of the times, England conducted itself as a civilised country, though the people occupying the lower end of the economic scale did not exactly operate by its rules, perhaps unwittingly. Racial sensitivities could be easily aroused. My home now lay not half a mile from Ridley Road, where Sir Oswald Mosley's cohort of Blackshirts hurled rhetorical brimstone from a soapbox almost every evening, specifically it seemed in my direction. Now I underwent a metamorphosis, justifying all the dreariness and hardship of army life.

A private soldier suffered few inhibitions. He barely possessed a name in that period of mass recruitment. Thankfully, I was now mostly distinguishable by my regimental number, medical category and incapacity to remain motionless during an officer's inspection on the parade ground. Inoculated against every known disease, issued with a real gas mask (not the stupid thing civilians carried in a cardboard box), I realised I was important to the War Department for manifestly it wanted me to live. Following recruit training, Whitehall posted me along with the 23rd Northumbrian Division to France. Civilisation was now safe.

History, arch-neutraliser of the inexplicable, speaks of the era as the phoney war, with the British forces steadfastly lined up before the Franco-Belgian frontier and the tranquillity rarely disturbed, except by the weather. BBC war correspondents stifled their yawns in twittering mellifluous nothings over the radio. We built fortifications of a sort, but at a speed that would have earned my gang of navvies in the London parks instant dismissal.

For several weeks we did not so much as hear a German aeroplane. The enemy surely never saw one of ours, for we had few to spare for this moribund 'Western Front'. There had been German victories in Poland, in Finland and Norway, while we experimented with French wines and gazed at the stars. It might have been the inauguration of another Hundred Years War, and no more decisive. For the rest, until 10 May 1940, my mind is a blank. That date rated as an important day for both Winston Churchill and myself. He became Prime Minister, while I saw a dead body for the first time in my life. The god of war had by then raised the safety curtain separating us, the spectators in khaki uniform, from them, the

5. Alfred, Emanuel and Barnet Litvinoff in 1940

6. Pinkus Litvinoff in 1942

7. Sylvia Litvinoff in the British Army in 1942, before her husband's capture in the Western Desert

8. The author, just disembarked from the *Orduña* troopship in Ismailya, July 1941

Dunkirk on my Mind

German ground forces in their tanks and those up above raining down murder from the skies.

Saw a dead body? I was detailed to clamber over an exploded railway bridge and help remove a statuesque figure seated astride a girder. I recall the difficulties we had releasing the body. I have no recollection of the soldier's face. But completing the picture in still life, as I relive the moment, there rested on that girder also an open bully-beef tin and a half-eaten packet of hard tack, both immune from electrocution.

The noteworthy point of this episode came next. We extricated the stiffening corpse and brought it down, to discover that nobody was available to receive this British soldier fallen in the line of duty. For as if by a signal, all France appeared on the move, and carrying in its stream half the population of Belgium, including conscripts who were still attired in First World War uniforms. Soldiers with and without rifles, civilians young and old, private cars surmounted with mattresses to protect their occupants from air gunners, bicycles, cats and dogs, they transformed the roads into swiftly flowing rivers of panicky life. Something warned me, as we buried the engineer beside the structure now constituting his tomb, that the army in which I served humble membership was already defeated.

I had not been informed, and years passed before I would read of it, that the 23rd Division, supported by two armoured brigades and apparently commanded by a certain General Franklyn, were defending a salient in the north-eastern corner of France. You could have fooled me. It also happened that General Rommel was on the advance just a few miles away, another matter of which I was happily oblivious. Had the German general despatched a reconnaissance to test out the line, it would have secured a good view of our backs.

How did one realise that one's army was already defeated? By an unmistakable sign. The quartermaster, who would previously guard with his life every miniscule portion of stores, demanding a signed chit of paper for whatever he released, began distributing his largesse like a drunken Father

A Very British Subject

Christmas. New boots, tins of fruit, bottles of rum, there they lay for the taking. You gathered them all, thanking the QM for this unwonted generosity, until their weight encumbered your step, raised a sweat and pulled you down. Before very long I stripped myself of all possessions except my water bottle and an iron ration of bitter chocolate.

Soon the 23rd Northumbrian Division assumed the character of a tribe of motorised bedouin trying to weave a path through the exhausted civilians crowding the roads. They were making for Paris, we were on our way to Dunkirk, yet we all seemed to be moving in the same direction. Enemy planes swooped low, strafing one and all with fire. Periodically we rested, to enable the cooks to pass round some skilly and allow our officers to scrutinise their maps. The latter operation created an impression somewhat of Christopher Columbus as he guessed his route across the Atlantic to the New World. Before 1940 average Tynesiders had not customarily visited France; they were strictly Scarborough holiday-makers. The only French they knew included the words Mademoiselle from Armentières. The civilians shuffled on, the most distraught among them occasionally stopping to beg food or water.

At one such halt a Geordie corporal beckoned me over. 'What's this bloke saying?' he asked. I went across. The 'bloke', elderly and haggard, appeared totally lost in the storm. He threw me a fleeting glance, then stared, producing in me a sensation that wills of itself and yet can arrive with reluctance. The man had stripped me of battledress to disclose the stigmata of ancient lineage in some East European location where his forefathers and mine shared a culture and a fate. He had recognised a fellow-Jew. The man needed a drink, and asked for it in a language then commonly spoken by the older generation of Belgian Jews, Yiddish. Silently I passed him my water-bottle – silently because I felt ashamed at being part of a military machine that had failed to protect him.

Now, I have never regarded my face as my fortune, but the incident left me wondering. Why had the corporal summoned *me*, of all the men in our outfit, to assist this straggler out of the refugee stream? Of course, the answer was obvious, shattering a fond illusion that as a soldier with a mere army number for precise identification I was no different from my comrades, just one of the lads. This had as little to do with anti-Semitism as being the odd goat in a herd of sheep. The corporal had no particular attitude towards me. It was merely that his was the wiser head, recognising that my face told a history different from the rest.

Since the heavens belonged to the Luftwaffe, we snailed our way into Dunkirk to find the docks ablaze. Unable to reach the harbour itself because all access roads were clogged with military transport, we joined a perplexed mass of creeping soldiery, a behemoth without a brain. With the military chain of command shattered, a unit deprived of instructions as to what to do next might just as well be asleep. It was now 28 May, and the benumbed British Expeditionary Force was abandoning its arms and vehicles and taking to the sands a mile or so east of flaming Dunkirk. Nightfall found us spread-eagled there, while daybreak signalled itself with regular visitations from enemy planes.

The official report (government editors work at their own pace, and this appeared as *Supplement to the London Gazette*, 17 October 1941) wrote of 'The Plan for Withdrawal', as though everything proceeded according to some ingenious strategic concept. The war books still quote from that document when describing the retreat, for it bears a resplendent martial title, thus: 'Despatch from General the Viscount Gort, VC, KCB, CBE, DSO, MVO, MC'. He must have commanded some other army. In truth, what had begun as a shambles turned into a rout baptised one day as a miracle.

Presumably every soldier who made it safely back across the Channel had his personal Dunkirk story, each at some negotiable distance from the facts. My memory of that experience again connects with a feeling of anonymity exploded. We regularly waded out to the ships. Owing to constant dive-bombing they dared not tarry, and in our thousands we just as regularly waded back again, drying quickly in the sun of that torrid summer during the day but shivering with cold at night. Few of the famous little boats had as yet joined in the rescue.

Military discipline was forgotten as each one of us seized his chance to get away. I saw mine when a small naval pinnace approached the shallows. Wading towards it, the waves up to my chest, I clutched the side. A corpulent sailor shouted into the wind, no doubt innocently, as he regarded my weather-beaten face sprouting three days of stubble. I can see to this day his stretched naval jersey as he called: 'We're only taking British boys!' Well, I was a British boy, and clambered aboard. But in the name of the good Lord 'Gort', why fling this at *me*?

These are tales, you might think, told by an East End working-class idiot. But having begun, I must finish. We landed at Ramsgate, where a sweet old lady spoke reassuringly to us as she passed mugs of hot tea round. 'Don't worry, boys', she said. 'It'll be over by Christmas.' The heartening words appeared to fall on deaf ears, until a Scottish comrade muttered: 'In that case we'll all be giving the Nazi salute.'

One year after Dunkirk I was deposited by the fates in collusion with the brass hats into the Western Desert, anonymous once more. The dreaded Rommel waited to pounce again, this time from the other side of the Gazala line in Libya. For me, part of the Eighth Army, the result was another ignominious defeat, and a yearning for the green fields of Hackney from the depths of a prison camp.

Returning to these shores almost five years to the day after the last time, I arrived at a reception centre to be fed, disinfested, graded and brought before the officer-in-charge of debriefing. He inspected the motley assortment of clothing I had accumulated in the course of a three-year captivity that had terminated in Poland, and scrutinised my face intently.

'Are you British?'

Not an offensive question, yet it told more than it asked. Had I not been British I would have enlisted in some other army, been liberated from some other Stalag, flown in some-

Dunkirk on my Mind

one else's plane to some other country. The officer waited patiently. He had been primed about ex-prisoners. One went easy with them. 'Are you British?'

'Yes,' I replied stonily. The war was over. I was a Jew again.

5 • The Cruise of the Orduña

She must have made a fine picture in her livery of the Pacific Steam Navigational Company, out of a world most of us knew only from illustrated magazines, or the cinema. Staring at her from the dockside, no great imagination was required to conjure up her history: the sounds of pre-war jollification, the clatter of sterling silver upon best quality napery, as she proudly performed during earlier years. In those days her 15,000 tons sailed regularly from Liverpool through the Panama Canal to the western side of South America, elegant Rudolph Valentino country.

Now she stood silent in the blacked out Clyde estuary. Those port-holes across there could well have belonged to the first class saloon. I could almost hear the swish of pale blue satin caressing light dancing pumps to the lilting Show Boat melodies of the 1930s.

'Ambrose and his orchestra, or maybe Harry Roy', observed a sardonic corporal. My musical knowledge was superior. 'Those bands only sailed in the best, like the *Queen Mary*', I corrected him. The *Orduña* came somewhat lower down the scale. Of course the corporal knew as much, but what harm a slight exaggeration to make a wry point?

'What d'you think, sar'nt-major?' the corporal asked that wise man, matured by the experience of 15 years in the Territorial Army. 'It'll be a cruise', replied Sergeant-Major Brusted, naturally referred to as Mr Bastard. We knew he was lying by the huskiness of his voice. It was May 1941. The

The Cruise of the Orduña

Orduña, seemingly suspended from a low cloud by her single funnel, was dressed in battleship grey. We had been balancing our weight, or sitting on our packs, for three hours. Without a drink, hot or cold. German U-boats could be depended upon to sink 100,000 tons of shipping in the North Atlantic every single week.

Movement orders had brought some 3,000 of us trucking up from Somerset to the Clyde. We had sweltered in our greatcoats down south. Now we buttoned up tight against the biting Scottish winds. We had not been formally told where we were bound (assuming that even our officers knew), but the pith helmets strapped to our packs, like humps upon a camel, gave the secret away. Patchily discoloured from storage since the previous world war, they were intended to prevent sunstroke. Obviously, we were destined for the Middle East. Getting those packs on and off with the helmets attached involved help from a comrade. Since Somerset I had found myself in cohabitation with Private Logan for this mutual service.

Much equipment travelled with us. Ammunition, ambulances, miles of cabling for signals, motor-cycles, lorries, they all had to be loaded before we could step on board. Mine was a medical unit (and I blushed internally whenever compelled to admit it) which signified that most of our officers were doctors, while a fair sprinkling of corporals and sergeants had enlisted as conscientious objectors. The 'conchies', being as it were of uncomplaining temperament, and usually a cut above the rest in smartness and intelligence, made good NCOs.

It always struck me as bizarre, nevertheless, that men forced into the army under duress saw no objection to being promoted over our heads. We formed part of a North Country infantry division of shop assistants, coal miners, dockers, transport drivers. Even in the Medics not a few of these northerners were near-illiterate. They drafted you in unsorted bundles to the Medics, in my case because I wore glasses, in another because their names happened to come out of the lottery at a moment when a division was below strength in that regard. Not infrequently we suffered ugly jeers: 'RAMC – Rob All My Comrades!'

After an eternity of waiting on shore they organised us for embarkation: every man, his pack, his kitbag, his water-bottle (empty) and both his helmets – steel against metal, canvas against heat. Then they hurried us up the *Orduña*'s gangways. Pressure of flesh coagulated into an endless giant centipede crawling into the vessel's innards, which were already populated by other khaki centipedes. First stop had to be the toilets, the original ones still signposted as *Señoras* and *Caballeros*, belonging to the time when those Spanish words really meant what they said. Needless to relate, they were now single-sexed, with cubicle doors open wide to accommodate the rush of the centipedes' booted feet, usually four at a time. Supplementary toilets, further below, were of more rudimentary construction and carried no signs. The best jobs on the vessel would go to the soldiers detailed to keep them clean. This labour went unsupervised by a bossy NCO. Sanitation orderlies customarily took their time.

More hours were consumed in stowing the troops into that half of the *Orduña* allocated to them. Our quarters for the next six weeks would be situated in every nook that previously had served second-class passengers for storage, or as bars, restaurants and recreation rooms. High ceilings had been rendered down to create layers of communal eating-sleeping-living areas, like extra shelving in some monster cupboard. Each man had his own place, for part of the day at least. He slept in a hammock slung above the table he sat at for his meals, and on which another man would be spending the night. In those early days of the war the Army Catering Corps was still in gestation, and four times a week the cooks produced stewed rabbit for dinner, on the other days a distasteful fish that went straight through the port-holes. Salmonella had not yet been invented.

In this space, until we discovered our sea legs, we indulged our every whim: played cards, nursed sea-sickness, wrote letters, read books and talked the hours away. No one

The Cruise of the Orduña

ventured into the open air during the first week, except for those passionate for a cigarette or when some busybody in authority ordered lifeboat drill. But simply to gaze on to the Atlantic? You'd be mad, so cruelly did the gales lash your face. Surely, in peacetime, nobody actually crossed this ocean for pleasure!

The other half of the *Orduña*, out of bounds to the ranks, was allocated to the officers, all 350 of them, those ranking below major having to make do with two sharing a cabin. Were the *Orduña* to strike a mine, or nose into the orbit of a U-boat, the sea would accept us all in an equal class of ocean wave, rank notwithstanding. Officers and men taken together came under the overall command of W.J. English, an elderly infantry colonel slumped in his cabin through some debility and as yet unavailable for duty. Having won his Victoria Cross in the Boer War, he suffered maladies garnered in long years of military service.

The soldier's life was ruled by a sacred text. Called Part One Orders, these were typewritten on a quarto sheet posted on the notice-board every evening. Traditionally, Part One Orders announced the dress proper for first parade the following day. It could be steel helmet or forage cap, full equipment or light equipment, running strip for a cross-country drag, etc. Then the hour of inspection was stated, and the roster for fire picquet detail as well as other individual duties. All this represented fulfilment of the thesis that nothing worked so crisply and unambiguously as the British Army, every man aware of his appointed station.

On Sundays, Part One Orders notified the time of the church parade and whether this one was designated voluntary or compulsory. A soldier had rights. According to the Army Act of 1908, administered without a syllable altered since the days of the great reformer Haldane, a Catholic could not be compelled to attend a church parade conducted according to the Protestant confession. However, most compulsory church parades were roughly ecumenical; all attended the same service.

I was the solitary Jew in my unit but, still on dry land, I was once ordered on to a church parade because a padre had arrived unannounced. My sergeant encountered some difficulty in mustering a congregation of minimum size at short notice, due to the plethora of men with excuses for non-attendance. He required a few bodies to make up what is known in the Hebrew rite as a *Minyan*. I protested at being press-ganged, only to be told: 'You too, Litvinoff, you're about the only Christian in this outfit!' The sergeant was a devout believer from Yorkshire, and a conscientious objector.

On the *Orduña*, the most important item on Part One Orders stated: 'Smoking is strictly forbidden below decks.' Short of mutiny, lighting up anywhere except out in the open was deemed the most heinous offence, involving trial by a senior officer. Of course, fire was the danger. It could result in catastrophe given that in our half of the ship there could be no free movement. Wherever you walked you were bumped, squeezed, tripped up, overtaken by another human being.

Five days out and fire did occur on the *Orduña*, discovered at night. The alarm (a Klaxen horn) produced a brief explosion of panic. Thankfully, our heartbeats swiftly resumed their normal pace. Friction, not carelessness or enemy action, was the culprit – combustion of the motor-bikes stored too tightly in one of the holds. They had rubbed against each other in tune with the motion of the ship, emitting more smoke than flame. Our fire picquet duties, ten yards between each man, covered every cranny of the upper levels of the *Orduña* while the holds, till then, had been neglected.

Another command of Part One Orders related to one's life-jacket. You were never to be separated from it. Up for air on deck, visiting the *caballeros*, queuing for meals, that life-jacket came too, the prudent, silent companion of all your movements. As the voyage proceeded it assumed the character of a bodily outgrowth, another limb. On life-boat drill we tied the thing around ourselves. The effect was the reverse of reassuring. One might trust one's lifebelt while loosely carrying it; but worn, it suggested no match in a possible contest against the North Atlantic breakers.

The skilled personnel keeping the *Orduña* afloat were exclusively civilian, men of the merchant navy. They went their separate way at a standard required to satisfy the seamen's trade union in war as in peace, and received wages that included a bonus for 'danger money'. We soldiers generally regarded them as a hostile force, a sentiment that was warmly reciprocated. We never saw the crews' quarters – off-limits again – and they enjoyed a reserved section of the decks. Contact between us was rare, except that these civilians ran the bar, sold the cigarettes and chocolate and even manned a corner cubby-hole termed the library. They could produce a variety of luxuries – soap and perfumed toiletries, biscuits, girlie publications, an apple, always setting their own fancy prices. Some of them let it be known that they were in the market for a deal with any soldier ready to sell a surplus pair of boots, or one of those army issue woollen sweaters.

No one flourished in wartime so much as a civilian engaged in monopoly trading with the army. On the *Orduña* this amounted only to small-scale racketeering. The crew charged what the traffic would carry for beer, the consumption of which rose sky high. Visiting the canteen entailed considerable stamina. It could accommodate a dozen fairly comfortably at the bar, though we patronised the little oasis on the ocean with the scuffle and fury of a riotous mob. Whatever you succeeded in passing over to the bartender earned you a beaker of liquid that bore little connection to a standard measure or a regulation brew. All the money travelled in the one direction; small change was neither proffered nor expected.

Doubtless some seamen had skilled duties relating to actual navigation, in the engine room, working the instruments, winding ropes. But we rarely, if ever, connected with any but the entrepreneurs purveying the mundane articles necessary for human existence. The army, one might think, was the provider of all things; not if you needed a comb, or a bootlace, or a toothbrush.

However, one other member of the crew whom I had the privilege of meeting was the ship's printer. He was a hangover from other days, for his principal function appeared to focus on the production of the daily menu scrutinised by the military Brahmins occupying the luxurious half of the *Orduña*. Officers' meals were not doled out to them in their rectangular mess-tins but served on china plates by uniformed waiters in white gloves. This we learned from the company batmen, whose servility in the presence of their officers turned to spite, treachery and gossip behind their backs.

One of the batmen informed me of the printer and his particular sideline. At a price he could produce headed writing paper for all comers, irrespective of rank. Just your name, regiment and number, naturally, if you wished to pass the censorship. As an incipient unpublished author I yearned to see my name in print. Call it a young man's affectation, but I fell for the headed notepaper. For a small additional charge the printer would place the sheets in a plywood case specially tailored to the purpose. I used a single sheet before being seized by the vanity of the exercise, whereupon I discreetly dropped the bulky lot into the sea.

To begin at the beginning, many of us, myself included, had not as yet tasted the stewed rabbit, nor sampled the dubious concoction described as beer, nor yet had I discovered the existence of the *Orduña*'s printer. During that first week we were totally uninterested in anything except the condition of our stomachs, and the unreliability of our legs – not so much sea-sickness as a general failure of bodily co-ordination. I tried worming my way towards the decks, only to be driven below again by the merciless weather. The condition did not render me unavailable for fire picquet – two hours on, two off, eight hours altogether. My name appeared beside Private Logan's.

He was now practically my soul-mate, an alphabetical accident. We had hardly spoken in Somerset, but by this time a relationship had developed. When we formed up for parade we stood together (sixth and seventh from the left-hand marker) and we virtually merged into a single organism in the centipede. Georgie Logan, already old for active service at about 32 years of age, was a regular soldier with nine years marked on his service record. Unmarried, and without a home of his own in civvy street, his face gave the impression of being composed from a multitude of meat pies consumed in a hundred NAAFI canteens. The hours that man had spent drinking tea while reading *Reader's Digest* in YMCAs in distant corners of the globe decorated with the Union Jack! Logan had sailed in troopships before, but this was wartime, rather different.

Regular soldiers of long service who had never risen beyond the rank of private constituted, in general, a breed all their own, cheated from birth. The king's shilling had been their lifeline during the depression years of the 1930s, when they languished at the bottom of the pile. Logan had travelled the globe, but ask him about Hong Kong or Malta, the West Indies or Cairo, and he blinked uncomprehendingly. Those colonial stations evoked few recollections of imperial splendour to him. Army barracks were the same the world over. Patronise one brothel and you'd have patronised the lot. Even the NAAFI employees were the same, for they followed the troops around. Wogs, Logan would declare, were no different anywhere – dead lazy thieving bastards. And while regular army officers might indulge in a chukka of polo for their recreation, buck privates of Logan's ilk spent their leisure crouched around a pack of cards or sleeping off their drink.

He had a lisp, and a perpetual drip about his nostrils. His vocabulary was restricted virtually to one expletive, a word that now spills casually from the mass of humanity, regardless of sex, occupation or location on the social scale – bullshit. Parades he described as 'bullshit', and lectures on the perils of venereal disease; protective measures to be adopted in the event of gas attacks, equally so. Bullshit was what you were expected to eat, as was any statement by any NCO, not to mention the extra gloss with which a soldier was exhorted to endow the toecaps of his boots. And if Logan cherished an opinion of significance on any subject, conformist or otherwise, he kept it strictly to himself. He spoke in broad Lancashire, castigating as bullshit any other accent from simple cockney to that flat vocalisation generated by NCOs in their constant repetition of drill commands on the parade ground.

Private Logan was not to be underestimated. Being more or less taciturn, he had developed the knack of offending absolutely no one. He neither shirked from duties assigned to him nor volunteered for any. Logan wasted no breath in a barrack-room argument and was innocent of transgressing army regulations or uttering the merest heresy. He invariably arranged to be the last man on parade without actually turning up late. Metaphorically, if in no other sense, he kept his nose clean. Later, the solitary disastrous occasion in the Western Desert when our company operated in an action against the enemy, with surviving members of the unit taken prisoner by General Rommel's Afrika Korps, found Logan safely behind the lines. He had contrived, some days before, to report sick on some undiagnosable complaint.

Logan and I took up our positions for fire picquet at a companion-way leading to the hatches, he above, myself below. It was past midnight, with both of us at our lowest ebb. The important responsibility of remaining erect, all senses alert for the slightest spark or the faintest odour of burning, lay beyond our competence. The *Orduña* protested violently against its treatment by the heavy seas, rocking precariously. My fellow-picquet and I, reduced by fatigue and physical discomfort to incapacity, held our ground steadfastly for the first half hour or so nevertheless. The orderly officer and sergeant of the guard could arrive at any instant on their round of inspection.

When exactly that transpired I have no recollection, for I had sunk ignominiously to the floor, lotus position, and fallen into a deep sleep. A noise woke me – the noise sergeants usually emitted when addressing the ranks in the presence of a superior officer. This took the nature of a snarling roar, similar to the sound long deemed essential in bayonet practice.

The Cruise of the Orduña

Enough said. There followed a dressing down, the laborious scratching of pencil on pad, my face downcast in contrition, and eventually the deduction of four days' pay and an entry on my Army Conduct Sheet (form 252) that would trail me to the end of my military career. In truth, this was a mild penalty for the crime of sleeping on duty, 'prejudicial to good ordah and military discipline, con'rary to Section 40 of the Army Act'.

But Logan? That instinct of old sweats for survival, much admired by Kipling, came to his rescue. He too had been asleep, though not in the lotus position. Using his belt, he had strapped himself perpendicular to a rail. Roused by the stentorian sergeant he met the enemy proudly upstanding. The orderly officer hurried on with barely a glance in his direction.

Our course described a wide arc over the North Atlantic, steering, it was calculated at that time, beyond U-boat range. The sea continued rough and the effective functioning of our legs, together with our stomachs' tolerance of the diet, was long in coming. We rendezvoused with several other troopships in deep water, one of them the stately *Georgic* of the Cunard-White Star Line. She displaced 28,000 tons. By the standards of Britain's senescent fleet of ocean-going liners, the *Georgic* was still young. Comforting to the eye, the troopships were being watched over by a flotilla of destroyers and a heavily armoured cruiser, the *Exeter*.

It was not then the practice of the army to burden the ranks with operational details, but we surmised that our convoy was now complete. Henceforth, it would proceed full steam ahead, to reinforce the command of General Auchinleck in the Middle East theatre. Auchinleck was winning few laurels in the clashes across the featureless blanket of sand between Alexandria and Benghazi. Mercifully, we remained ignorant of Winston Churchill's current topmost preoccupation: not the ding-dong in the desert but the emergence in the North Atlantic of Germany's newest battleship, the *Bismarck*, out hunting in the company of a cruiser, the *Prinz Eugen*, likewise put in recent commission. The colonel described as 'OC

Troops' on the *Orduña* had still not shown his face anywhere to the men under his rule.

Shortly after the kindling of our motor-bikes into brief flame, to bring sickening cognisance of the unexpected ways a crowded community might die when travelling over water a thousand fathoms deep, we grew fit enough to take better note of our surroundings. Space to stretch limbs was available in those portions of the decks accessible to the ranks. We learnt to harmonise our movements to the roll of the vessel. The ocean itself, mysterious and cunning and violent though it still remained, lost its constant menace.

Men ceased bumping into each other, tore the skin off their shins less frequently, slept more deeply. Humankind began, as it were, to reveal a kinder side. The beer flowed copiously, draining a week's pay in hours, and yet drunkenness was rare. In a surge of resolution I started on *Anna Karenina*, borrowed from the ship's library of Penguin editions. My life had hitherto passed Tolstoy by unregarded.

Each day brought the minor occurrences that made for conversation as, buttoned up tight, we could dare the weather to do its worst: a corporal of the Northumberland Fusiliers attempting suicide with a razor-blade; a ration of beef to interrupt the monotony of regular rabbit; and a heavy-throated rendering of 'Danny Boy' at an impromptu singsong. Not often would a British squaddie risk the derision of his comrades with a solo performance.

On three consecutive days we came on deck to be entertained by the aerobatics of the solitary aircraft escorting the convoy. Presumably a Swordfish, it catapulted expertly from our flagship. The plane made a heart-warming sight. It flew around each vessel, leapt somersaults, rose high to the clouds one moment, almost brushing the waves the next. In appreciation of the brave display we greeted the pilot's exhibitions with cheers.

Up he ascended to the skies on the fourth of his daily spectaculars. Higher and higher, a loop achieved, a circuit of the convoy, and he was already homing on swift wing through a descending hypotenuse. Suddenly the aircraft burst into flames – some mechanical fault, no doubt, as no enemy was in evidence. Within seconds the sea covered the pilot and his plaything of a kite. That was the last we knew. The convoy sailed on. Anyway, the bugle called for dinner just then, and silently we made our way below. By the afternoon the incident no longer occupied our talk, probably not our thoughts either.

The war? It seemed hardly to concern itself with our convoy. We discussed it desultorily, as though the issue would be decided on some other planet. Little by way of news reached us, wireless being exclusively in the possession of those who required it for their duties. A drift occasionally percolated, in laconic straggles of information via a member of the crew. 'There's been another push up the desert', say, or 'London's copped it again'. I became immersed in the vagaries of Vronsky's affair with Anna Karenina.

The *Orduña* continued steaming west, chasing the sunset. 'Greenland will be somewhere over there.' An infantry man from the Hartlepool fishing fraternity knowingly volunteered the information. None of his hearers presumed to contradict him. 'Or maybe Iceland', he reckoned.

We knew he was right when word passed through the ship on 24 May that at no great distance from our convoy, measured in oceanic terms, a battle was in progress, and not going well for Britain. By the same evening we had become aware of the *Bismarck*'s presence, notified by the sinking of the largest warship in our or any other navy, the battle-cruiser *Hood*. She had disappeared within minutes, they said, with all hands lost, something approaching 1,500 men – as many as died when the unsinkable *Titanic* went down on her maiden voyage. The wireless indicated how the *Bismarck* had caught up with the *Hood*. Or was it the other way around?

The British, at this stage of the war, were inured to defeats: Poland conquered in just a few days; our men scurrying out of Narvik, then Dunkirk; France knocked out of the action. We had left the Clyde to the intelligence that the Jerries had got the better of us in Greece, too. Battleships had gone down before the *Hood* – did we have any left? However, all that constituted war in the abstract. One read about it, talked a little, and then proceeded on another ordinary day. Some of us had experienced the terrors of the beach at Dunkirk, but that was a year ago.

But for all who sailed on the *Orduña* and the rest of our convoy, the *Bismarck* brought the war right to the pit of our stomachs. She must be lurking somewhere out there in our waters. That day none of our escort vessels, the destroyers or the cruiser, were to be seen. They had left us orphaned in the Atlantic, to go in pursuit of the *Bismarck*. We yearned to feel the dry land of North Africa under our feet.

But it was alright! Good old Winnie! Trust the Royal Navy! Within the space of 72 hours the *Bismarck* itself lay beneath the waves. The nightmare was over. Georgie Logan never said a word. He gave no hint of fear at the sinking of the *Hood*, no release of delight at the ending of the *Bismarck*. I'm not convinced he was completely aware of the implication of the two events. Possibly it was all bullshit to him.

Another week out and the convoy turned southward, into warmer air. Our escort vessels never returned, so we deduced that we now voyaged out of enemy range. The sunshine loosened tongues. Officers appeared more frequently among us, to exchange a joke or utilise a little of the navigational jargon gathered in the first-class compartment concerning the vessel's peculiarities and her speed. They had also picked up scraps of her history. The *Orduña*, named after a river in Peru, had sailed on her maiden voyage in 1914 just before the First World War, intending to be the first passenger liner through the Panama Canal, when an American vessel jumped the gun. In normal times she plied the Atlantic after first visiting Spanish ports, and was thus a welcome visitor to harbours along the Pacific coast.

More to combat tedium than for any serious purpose, we watched demonstrations of men dismantling and reassembling a bren gun. They demonstrated wearing a blindfold, then a gas mask. We were given a course in Morse code. As Medics,

The Cruise of the Orduña

my unit brushed up on first aid (yet again), exercising with that venerable RAMC standby, the Thomas splint. The contraption had been devised to reduce pain and alleviate shock from a fractured leg under battlefield conditions. Once only in the desert would we actually use the complicated splint. It was on a fighter pilot injured during a forced landing. He died nevertheless.

Some bright spirit organised a spelling bee on the *Orduña*, in emulation of the contests introduced by the BBC at home pending the creation of such light fare as 'The Navy Lark' and 'The Army Game' during the languid early days of the war. Our spelling bee matched officers against other ranks. I was chosen, and made my usual blunder of parading my smidgen of education where this was most liable to offend. I tactlessly challenged our Captain Lorimer, a doctor in military disguise, to spell 'eleemosynary'. He threw me a glance approaching disgust. He'd never heard of the word, Lorimer protested, suggesting it didn't exist. I assumed he must be thinking: 'That too-clever show-off again.' He would have been right. I earned no laurels throughout my active service career, not one pathetic chevron as lance-corporal. Really intelligent soldiers, understanding the workings of the power structure, pulled themselves up in the hierarchy through a winning servility. They supervised the dirtiest jobs rather than performed them.

Sergeant Holmes gave me a wink. 'Never you mind', he whispered. 'I've a copy of Fielding's *Tom Jones* in my kitbag. If he really wants to know, he can find "eleemosynary" in the opening paragraph.' However, Holmes, the soul of discretion, said nothing to the captain.

We had voyaged some 3,000 miles by this time, yet Colonel English, Boer War VC and veteran of other battles long ago, had still not materialised as our commander. We now learned why. The colonel had died, in his bed, the gentle death of an old warrior recalled to the colours for his third war. He had become cargo, deposited in the holds awaiting a permanent resting place in some corner of an Egyptian field that was forever England: a military cemetery beside the Suez Canal. If ghosts can haunt ships as they are reputed to haunt old mansions, then Colonel English surely received merited promotion in death as the ghost of the *Orduña*.

Of infinitely greater interest to the troops, a sight presented itself to break the remorseless engagement of sea with sky. We observed a faint vista of Africa, soon a brown coastline and, suddenly, trees. *Tierra, tierra*! Christopher Columbus had cried centuries earlier. Our excitement could well have equalled his. We were approaching Freetown, in Sierra Leone. As if invoked by old Neptune himself, the waters erupted with human voice. We were being welcomed to port by a fleet of baby canoes from which young blacks shouted 'Heh, Tommy!' Demonstrating their diving skills, they begged money. So this was what Churchill unfailingly summoned in his morale-raising speeches: the Empire. Hitherto, most Britishers knew of their overseas possessions only through the red blobs on the map, together denoting a brotherhood of passionate loyalty to the benign Mother Island.

Freetown proved a spectacle indeed, though here the Empire was for admiring from afar, not to be trodden upon. The bustling port seemed rather like a circus. The boys clowned in the water for coins (large bright ones only, florins and half-crowns), while business of a more serious nature, evidenced by stores discharging, bicycles wheeling, hooters blaring, fascinated our hungry eyes.

Motor cars cruised up and down the landing stages on errands that bespoke international importance. Bouncing officials in tropical kit huffed and puffed about the place, the outcome of the war depending upon every scrap of paper they brandished. And for the inhabitants, black or white, of what had lately been a sleepy colonial outpost, the troopships brought physical contact with the nation they regarded, for the present at least, as master of the cosmos.

Those on the convoy could now feel their lives being renewed. We had safely run the gauntlet of the perilous North Atlantic. Henceforth we would sail with the coast of Africa always in view. Should a U-boat stray so far from base as to sink the *Orduña*, it could not send us all down to Davy Jones's locker – not where innumerable fishing vessels manned by plucky little subjects of the British Empire splashed about. They would surely die themselves rather than observe the defenders of their liberty perish. The entire length of coastline? Well, no one else counted in Africa, of that we were convinced. The French were finished, weren't they, while Portugal was a neutral nothing. Churchill would not drive the Nazis from all this territory simply to give it back to lesser nations after the war.

Crossing the Equator we felt the itch of shore leave coming up at last, in loyal South Africa. Or was it merely the heat? Skin rashes made their appearance on our bodies now, notification that personal hygiene was not to be neglected, particularly by us Medics.

'Get yourselves some talcum powder, for your private parts', ordered a young lieutenant who had joined us direct from the wards of the Royal Victorian Infirmary in Newcastle. 'That's how mothers deal with their babies' wet bottoms.' We tittered. Talcum powder did not feature strongly as a personal necessity for the British male. We thought of it as an indulgence of decadent Latins. Still, I bought a box at our little shop, where a crew member had them piled high. The powder exuded the scent of bedrooms in civvy street. In applying it I was momentarily overcome by the pressure of blood in a sexual fantasy.

Anticipation of South Africa became tinged with anxiety. Who would be the unlucky ones who had to remain on board for guard duty? The *Orduña* could not be totally deserted, an open invitation to fire, or theft, or sabotage. And didn't those NCOs make a meal of it, with their threats! I almost wept with relief when the duty roster was posted on Part One Orders. Miraculously, my name was omitted.

We separated from the *Georgic* near the Cape. Other troop-ships ploughed ahead, apparently bound for India. It was evening when the *Orduña* steamed into Durban, which greeted us in a wondrous sparkle of light. In this fairyland the black-out curtain, mournfully covering every British city, was unknown. The next morning, Friday, 21 June, I was smartly rigged out, boots highly polished, conduct impeccable, as I descended to join the khaki stream making for the shops. I had till 23.59 hours to go where I wished, talk to anyone I pleased and eat a decent meal. Georgie Logan stalked my shadow. Determined we should not form a double act in this hemisphere, I took care to lose him.

I knew not a soul in South Africa, though a welcome radiated from virtually every pale Durban face. Enter a bar and you were handed a drink for nothing. Buy cigarettes or confectionary – no longer on display at home – and another customer would insist upon paying. Europeans walked the spotless pavements, blacks shuffled along the gutters.

The chasm separating the two races did not find me appalled. I had outlived the instinct, held faithfully in my teens, of crying 'Down with oppression, imperialism, this, that and the other!' Here, for the three days of my liberty, I intended to become a temporary imperialist myself, so as to make the most of colonial rule. One war at a time was enough, dammit. Knowing little of the Afrikaner question, it remained beyond my perception that a considerable proportion of Durban's white inhabitants acknowledged no interest in the outcome of the war, except to cherish the hope that Adolf Hitler would emerge the victor.

Soldiers with any degree of initiative, on arrival in a strange city, sought companionship among like-minded people. That way they assuaged loneliness, dropped their guard, found congenial chatter, ate in style. Believers were invariably drawn to the church of their denomination, philatelists to a stamp club, pigeon fanciers and amateur photographers to their own. True loners would inevitably drift to a pub or cinema, then maybe the YMCA, or respond to the blandishments of a sister of the *demi-monde* – sometimes all of these.

My method was to seek out a synagogue. Most large towns, in the far-flung empire as well as within the United Kingdom, boasted its Jewish community. Many a congregation in

The Cruise of the Orduña

England, Scotland and Wales have found me, a stranger, participating in evening prayers; and then rewarding my piety with an invitation to join some family's table. Certainly, none of them would send a son of the faith out into the cold on a Friday, the Sabbath Eve.

I had rarely, in civilian life, entered a synagogue. I had not been raised in a conformist family. My virtue in that regard developed from the exigencies of army service, to be fiercely confirmed by the revelation of God's bounty proffered here in Durban. The town constituted a terrestrial paradise: huge bunches of bananas decorating every fruiterer's window; chocolate, eggs, meat, all available in quantities to reduce a British ration-book to so much waste paper. After four weeks' diet of stewed rabbit washed down with a mug of stewed tea I had all but forgotten the colour, shape and smell of real food. A spring in my step, I explored the marvels of the city until the appropriate hour (dusk) that I calculated would bring Durban Jewry to their gaunt, red-bricked edifice for worship.

Entering the synagogue discreetly, I chose a seat at the back. Half empty as the place proved to be, I quickly detected that others from the troopship – three men in khaki – had found their way here, doubtless from an urge close to my own. As it happened, all were attired in the superfine serge complete with Sam Browne belt that proclaimed their dignity, caste and station – officers.

The Friday evening service is customarily brief, but this one dragged. Labouring at the Hebrew liturgy I stood when the congregation stood, sat when it sat. Some activity took place relating to the opening of the Holy Ark and withdrawal of the sacred scrolls reposing there. It is deemed an honour to participate in this ritual, and one of the officers, evidently familiar with the routine, was awarded the privilege. The assembly bowed in contemplation of God's mystery and majesty. Fervently I bowed in concert. Night was upon us. The Sabbath had arrived.

The service terminated at last, with a general shaking of hands and the benediction 'Good *Shabbos*' exchanged. Then the fraternity rapidly dispersed, each officer guest from Britain collected by a communal dignitary. A splendid feast surely awaited them in some mansion. No one volunteered to take the humble private seated obscurely on the rear benches, despite a few half-glances thrown in his direction. Eventually just one man and his wife remained. She gathered up the prayer books. He held the keys to the synagogue doors. No question about it, he was the congregation's beadle, secretary, and general purpose man.

Habitually in Jewish communities, the professional servant occupies a modest place. Durban was no exception. The man responsible for rounding affairs off hesitated. Our eyes met. Did I imagine his sigh or was it truly audible, before he asked: 'You from the troopship?' as if a stranger might have arrived from Mars. I nodded.

'We're Mr and Mrs Lewis. Would you care to come with us?' I was all respectful gratitude, of course, though not without a sardonic thought. A distinguished guest would render the Sabbath meal a domestic occasion, even a triumph. But a private soldier . . . ?

Theirs was a liberal congregation, stripped of antique shibboleths like proceeding on foot in recognition of the sanctity of the seventh day. We entered the car park. Among the remaining limousines I espied a vehicle belonging to the lesser breeds of the Morris stable. I knew it to be Mr Lewis's car before being directed there. On the way to their flat in the Berea we stopped off at a garage. 'Just do the tyres, please', he commanded the dark-faced menial, 'we're all right for petrol.' No coin by way of a tip passed hands, and off we sped. South Africa could be a land bloated with its wartime prosperity. Mr Lewis did not share in it.

Yet I had struck gold. By my experience the home appeared lavish, breathing harmony. The Lewises had two delightful, talkative daughters, about twelve and ten years of age. They wanted to hear about London. How large was it? Had I ever seen the king and queen? Was I married? But you look so young (I *was* young). What's the name of your wife? Taking in the scene and finding my voice, I thoroughly enjoyed being the celebrity at the feast. A plump black servant waited at table.

'Why don't you come and live here after the war?' Mr Lewis asked. 'We so need people. British of course. Fortunes are being made in South Africa. You won't find a higher standard of living anywhere in the world.'

We met again the next day and drove out to the Valley of a Thousand Hills, myself squeezed in the back of the Morris between the chattering girls. This was another Africa, dusty, stark country. Powerful cars ate up the miles of road lined with heavily loaded pedestrians, black every one. We passed shanty villages, adults as well as children barefoot, an occasional beehive hut of the Zulus. A day and a half in this region, and I felt I could honestly declare I knew South Africa. They took me to the Indian market, with its pungent smells and dazzling colour. Here the people were better dressed, the women particularly, and quietly dignified.

On our return to Durban following the excursion into the country, the radio at the Lewises told of Hitler's invasion of Russia. We heard Churchill's historic speech promising all aid to the new Soviet ally. Then we drove over to the Durban Jewish Club, to drink coffee and discuss the exciting war news. A few men were in uniform and bore the shoulder flash of the South African forces. I sensed both the euphoria and the fear. The dread of this tiny English-speaking enclave was not of the coloured classes serving the coffee and mowing the lawns. The idea of them ever becoming a nation appeared inconceivable. It was the fear of the country's domination by the Afrikaners, who castigated a 'Hitler' in their own history, the British Prime Minister Lord Salisbury.

'The blacks are all right', Mr Lewis conceded. 'I certainly prefer them to the Indians.' No doubt. The negro alone was the true slave in these parts. Many Indians had education and joined the professions, too nearly equal to the whites for the latter's peace of mind amid their luxuries. Some day they could encroach.

The girls kept on with their questioning. 'Will you write to us when you are up North?' That's how South Africans referred to the Libyan battlefield. 'Oh, yes. But you must reply to my letters.' The girls wrote and wrote. So did I, while I could.

The ironies lay in the future. I did not emigrate to South Africa. But this little family came to England, the girls first. By then they had university degrees and good Jewish husbands. They had identified with the black people's cause, rendering them conspirators against the apartheid paradise. Their ageing parents followed. When the Afrikaners gained control England became the spiritual home of South Africa's Jews, with the State of Israel a close second.

We all trooped back to the *Orduña* as different men. The brief sojourn in a land of colonial plenty altered our understanding of riches and poverty from what we knew of it in England. Which was the reality, which the illusion? A soldier of my unit was inspired not only to compose a hymn of praise for Durban but dared to sing it to us on deck. Replete with banalities it might be, but we heard him out without a snigger. Half a dozen men deserted ship. How many made a private resolve to return after the war? My guess is that, glued to their northern shires, they dreamt nostalgically about Durban across the decades, until the day the man named Nelson Mandela appeared on their television screens.

No convoy now. The *Orduña* serenely ploughed the foam alone for the *Georgic* had forged ahead. Towards the end of the fifth week of the voyage we arrived at Aden. It was destined to be a longish stay. Listlessly, we stared at Arabia. That should have been all. From what we could descry, the place could not possess a great deal to rouse our curiosity. Yet the docking of the *Orduña* at Muslim Aden perhaps merits a note in Britain's rigid military history.

We soldiers had, for the last five weeks, suffered an unspeakable diet, accepted the fetid concentration of humanity as we ate, slept and whiled the tedium away – all without protest. That's how the system had worked for poor Tommy since his first salute to the being nearest to a god he would encounter on earth, and continued still. But at Aden a subtle change occurred on the *Orduña*.

Observing that the officers were escaping for shore leave, the men's sense of injustice found spontaneous voice. They let out a tremendous volley of boos. This was hardly a mutiny, to be sure, but never had I witnessed a like gesture of discontent with the gulf separating the 'gentlemen' from other ranks. Those officers could not but be aware of it themselves. We anticipated reproof, admonition, a lecture perhaps, from the NCOs, those intermediaries whose own authority survived through their studied implementation of the system. On the contrary, and to our amazement, many of them joined in the chorus of resentment.

In the event, protestation dissolved into another sound, derisive laughter this time, at the expense of that expertise, hitherto unassailed, of the seamen to whom we had entrusted our lives. During their respite at Aden from whatever tasks they regularly performed the crew were put to work releasing the lifeboats from their davits. The exercise was to test the boats' seaworthiness, never conducted during all the safety drills of the long voyage. The boats were lowered. Without exception, all of them rapidly filled with water and, before our astonished eyes, sank beneath the brine. Lifeboats!

Slow progress now: another week and we waited at Tewfik for our turn to be piloted through the Suez Canal, destination Port Said. The sea had lost its danger, and interest, for all three thousand of us. We had reached Egypt. Any further surprises due to take place, we reckoned, would occur on dry land. But what was that over there, across the little bay. It couldn't be . . . ? Yes, it was. The *Orduña*'s big sister, the sturdy *Georgic*, lay two-thirds under water. She had beaten us round the Cape, using her superior speed in a spurt forward. She was therefore on time for a rendezvous with a squadron of German bombers. Holed and set on fire, she offered shattering testimony to the accidents of war. How many died on the *Georgic* we never knew.

Gazing sorrowfully at what had been a fine vessel, a sailor

commented: 'They'll never get her afloat again.' He was wrong. As a civilian traveller I boarded her myself in New York, to enjoy a perfect voyage in the summer of 1950, all the way to Liverpool. It transpired that the *Georgic* outlived the *Orduña*, which was broken up for scrap in 1951. My tired troopship was reborn in a second vessel likewise named the *Orduña*. Bless those who sail in her. Bless 'em all.

6 • A Blind Date

'You missed a page out, Frank', Ben said. It served as an accusation.

The reader was angered at the interruption. Although he was speaking the words from his book out loud, his thoughts had escaped into a reverie, miles away. Thoughts were the only activity they could command at that time, the sole private occupation left. This was shortly after their capture in the desert campaign, Frank alone being blessed with sight in the group of six blind men. They lay on groundsheets in a large tent, almost a marquee, the flaps folded back to let the heat out and entice a breeze in. The sick bay, they called it.

The arrival of the Afrika Korps in Libya wiped the shine off the Desert Rats. Until then the campaign seemed more like a parade than a battle – up the blue from Alex to Tobruk and a thrust into Benghazi, soon transformed into a rollicking Australian playground. Then Rommel's panzers intervened. Taking over from the Italians the panzers promptly had the British on the run. In May of 1942 you couldn't see an Australian for dust: first into Benghazi, first out. At home Churchill declared that the Germans had no experience of desert warfare, all the disadvantages were piled high against them. That was rich. The way they carried their water and petrol was a revelation in itself, so cleverly devised that the British scrapped their own containers for those famous 'jerricans'.

The men of the Afrika Korps even possessed specially printed booklets of chess problems. No wonder they made mincemeat of the troops holding the Knightsbridge Box on the Gazala perimeter, where Ben and the others got blinded. Their attendant Frank was a medical orderly who had become entangled in a minefield that wasn't supposed to be there, until the enemy picked him up and he was performing his first-aid duties on the wrong side of the wire.

A front hardly applied in the desert. Action took the form of a war at sea, manoeuvring. Therefore it was comparatively simple to evade capture by removing oneself, sharply, from the battle. The wounded could escape too, if their legs held. But not the blind. When Ben and his comrades were shot up in their Matildas they were lucky to free themselves from the flaming tanks. Afterwards all they dared was to squat and stay still. Eyeless in Gazala, you might say.

Frank had been busy patching up arms and legs. During the lull preceding the Knightsbridge set-to he had assisted the MO in the underground casualty station. He took temperatures, made tea, gave blanket baths, applied clean dressings. Now, with these fellows, he felt changed into a wet nurse and hated the job. When captured, a soldier shares the mentality somewhat of a man dossing homeless under a bridge. He knows it doesn't really matter to anyone except himself whether he wakes or sleeps for ever. But what if the soldier is blind into the bargain?

The whole of Frank's day was wrapped up in his six: escorting them to the latrines, helping them to wash, sorting out their clothes (a man always knew he had the wrong vest, by its smell), or just talking to kill the hours. Frank realised they clung to the hope that their sight would return, once they reached a proper hospital with specialist doctors. 'I can just make out a minaret over there', Wally Smith had assured him, 'so it must be coming back.' Frank followed the direction but failed to find Benghazi's minarets, even with his good eyes.

The Germans had unloaded them from trucks on to this scrubby patch of Libyan desert, along with hundreds of other prisoners, virtually before the Italians completed erection of the barbed enclosure. Daytime they roasted, at night they froze. The tent was no field hospital in the way the Eighth

Army would set one up, with morphine and mattresses and its own plentiful supply of drinking water. The Ites were a real Fred Karno's army. Were it not for Rommel's lot old man Auchinleck would have been dining in Rome by this time.

Just now Frank ached to be rid of his charges. Their minds were like taut elastic ready to snap. Their needs were few, he admitted, but their demands persistent. If they asked for anything they wanted it so badly Frank just had to jump. He scrounged a shirt here and there from other prisoners, and books – thrillers usually for an easy read. Amazing, some of the possessions clutched by soldiers falling into the bag. One of them owned a clarinet and wore it slung over a shoulder even in the latrines in case it got lifted. Another entered captivity with half a dozen watches up his arm.

Luckily, the Ites had this human streak, at one moment taunting the British (many of them South African nancy-boys) for surrendering Tobruk without a fight, then moved almost to tears by the pathetic group Frank steered, Indian-file style, hand on shoulder, for some exercise in gaining confidence. The Ites sent a little 'Wog' boy from Benghazi to help Frank keep the work under. The boy called himself some name like Zachary. He cleared up about the place, nothing anyone else willingly did, because capture in the desert usually began with a heavy attack of diarrhoea itching to turn into dysentery and draining a man's strength. Utterly sick of the situation, Frank only kept a grip on his temper with difficulty. To think most of his own outfit were safely away down the blue, tucked into the Mersah Matruh base!

They nicknamed the boy Johnny. He liked that, for it was what the natives called any man in British uniform when they made contact for trade, and took the soldiers to the cleaners. But he was different from the Cairo shoe-shine kids. He was a link with normality, that Johnny, beetling off home to Benghazi every evening while they had to stick it out, days into weeks.

The day Ben interrupted Frank's reading the strain was beginning to tell on them all. The sun burned fiercely from a cloudless sky and the story was dull – not a murder in the first dozen pages. Frank could barely keep his eyes open.

'You've missed a page out, Frank.'

'I haven't, you know, Ben. I've been reading straight on without turning over, so how could I?'

'It doesn't make sense. Have another look and see whether a page is missing. It's no good falling asleep if you're supposed to be reading to us.' Angry as Frank felt, he said nothing as he glanced over the page numbers. Sure enough, Ben was right. A sheet was missing. They ran from 12 to 15. (Worn-out paperbacks doubled as toilet paper.)

'With such a rotten story who care's if a bit's got lost.' This from Wally Smith, whose head bore the ravages of second degree burns. 'The more he leaves out the sooner we'll be shut of it. Frank's no reader anyway – he'd make *No Orchids* sound like a piece out of the Bible.'

'All right, lads', Frank said. 'I'll pack it in. You've had enough. I reckon we could all do with a wink of sleep.'

'The story's not that bad', Ben protested. 'I was quite enjoying it. Only you could put a bit more life into your reading, Frank.'

'Why don't you try doing it yourself', Wally snapped, his voice coming from half way under his blanket. 'Then we'll have less of your nagging and moaning.'

Taken each by himself, Frank found them fairly manageable. Together they were a mass of jealousies and conflicting resentments, liable to explode in a moment. Normal comradeship hung upon a thread of monosyllables. Frank knew Wally and Ben were both intent upon the last word of the argument.

'And don't make fun of the Bible, Wally.' It came in a hiss from Ben, the most nervy one. 'Some of us might actually respect what it says.'

Wally had regarded the incident as more or less closed. Now he turned in Ben's direction. 'Oh, so we've got a sky-pilot here, have we? Well, don't preach to me. The Bible's all fairy stories and hypocrisy. I'd sooner believe the stuff in a kid's comic.

A Blind Date

Ben, you can bury yourself in the Bible, with the rest of the rubbish that gets dished out as Christianity.'

'I'm not a Christian', Ben replied. 'I'm a Jew.'

'That explains it then. And you too.'

'What about a nice brew of the best Italian ersatz coffee?' Frank butted in wearily. 'Johnny's getting it ready, so we can save our throats and leave our souls for another time.'

'Arseholes, you mean', said Wally. Frank was worried, and fell to watching Johnny at work. Those two men were storing up their feelings for a proper bust-up.

Johnny was a really decent 'Wog'. He had an open look, and his wrinkle of a nose screwed up whenever someone noticed him – never passing a glance but always with a smile while he darted around trying to be helpful. He wore a skull cap like the rest of them, though his was a fairly extravagant affair intertwined with gold thread. For the rest, he appeared like all the other Libyans in his long white robe, which he covered with an army issue drill shirt with the cuffs flapping and a cavalry flash on the shoulder, discarded no doubt by a tankman in the last push. Johnny was very good to the lads around their camp, though he need not have been, because when you get captured you pretty well become a 'Wog' yourself. If he took a rest he spent it staring at the blind prisoners, fanning them and driving away the flies.

Frank observed that Johnny was frustrated with himself for not knowing a word of English. It was clear he would have wished to tell them how sorry he was that they were blinded, and that soon perhaps they would be sent to a proper hospital where a real doctor could operate and maybe give them their eyes back. Frank felt Johnny revealed some of the traits of a faithful dog.

The argument between Wally and Ben set Frank wondering about religion. One always encountered fellows in the army who carried a prayer book in their haversacks and spoke a tidy language. As a rule no one appeared to care enough, or discussed the rights or wrongs of this religion or that, to make a production out of it, with accusations and insults. Yet religious chatter had occurred here, causing a rift between men so pathetically afflicted, one couldn't help being cynical.

In the days following Frank had to watch himself. If he sat and talked with Wally for a while he made sure he did the same with Ben, and for an equal period of time. They were becoming a problem. If Ben needed to visit the latrines Wally could decide at that precise moment that he wanted a walk in the exercise area. When Wally suggested a brew-up Ben would automatically ask Frank to read something to him. They had begun to inhabit rival worlds. The other four noticed it too, and broke the endless tedium with pointless bickering, as though reminding Frank of their existence. More than Wally, Ben's nerves were approaching the edge.

He asked Frank the date. When told, he lay quiet without speaking. Uncomfortable minutes passed. Then he sobbed. They all succumbed for brief periods, but Ben sustained it. He was actually crying, like a child, without tears.

'What's wrong, Ben?' Frank enquired.

'Oh, forget it. You couldn't help.'

'Try me.' But Frank suspected that Ben wanted something not catered for in the stretcher-bearer's handbook. Ben mumbled about a special requiem his people had for the dead on certain occasions. He explained: 'We say this prayer called *Kaddish*, and a year ago my sister died in an air-raid. Nothing really, I know, but we do it.'

Frank guessed as much: some religious thing. He tried making light of it. 'I'd be only too ready to say your prayer here and now, Ben, in my best reading voice, if I knew what it was, and where to find it. But that would be a tough proposition in a hell-hole like this.'

'It's tougher than that', Ben replied, now on the point of laughing. 'You didn't learn Hebrew at school, did you, Frank, so I think it's a bit late to start now.' And he added: 'I can't say this kind of thing worried me in the past. Only now it's going to be different, not being able to see. It puts us all level, doesn't it, the whole lot of us, about God. No one's seen *him*.

A Blind Date

'And if you don't have this *Kaddish* for your sister it's going to be hard. Is that it, Ben?'

'Let's not talk about it.'

'Don't believe that sky-pilot stuff!' This was Wally, calling from his corner of the tent. 'Don't you believe him, Frank. If he cared that much for his religion he would know that one by heart. Even I know the Lord's Prayer, *and* a few others, though they've meant nothing to me since I was out of short trousers. What does he expect, a church parade? Ben's demanding preferential treatment, like all his clan. As bold as brass when they're all right, blubbering if they get hurt.' Wally was now at his provocative best, stirring it up as the mood took him.

'Come off it, Wall-ee!' Frank's rebuke emerged more as a plea. This was uncharted ground. 'It's all very well coming from you. Everybody sneaks off to the padre now and then, even the blokes against religion. Talking things out with the lads in trouble is part of the job. Who's Ben got here to understand what he's driving at? He wants someone to remember what he remembers. I suppose it's bloody lonely for him.'

Frank felt embarrassed by his role as nursemaid and referee. Lonely? They should know how it was with him, the only medical in the place, and detesting every sodding minute.

But nothing would stop Wally. 'Look here, didn't we drop into the same packet at Knightsbridge? Didn't we get hurt the same way, everything going black, and finish up in the same stinking mess? Now Ben's trying to make out he's different, moaning for what he can't have, and nor can I. It's not reasonable. He's no better than the rest of us.'

'I do know this prayer by heart, Wally. Only I want to hear it said for me. Like when you want a woman, you expect something to come from her lips too, a few love words, don't you?'

'Don't ask me. Back in Hull I wasn't old enough to have a woman.' This was beginning to sound foolish. However, another of them piped in, Charlie, a cockney in the East Kents. 'Well, when it happens, it'll be as close as you'll ever get to God, Wally', he said.

Evening had just passed across the camp, and all went quiet.

A Very British Subject

Fresh Italian sentries took up positions and shuffled around to stay awake. The sky emptied of the interminable drone of aircraft. Frank stood outside the tent. Why didn't our boys attack Benghazi from the sea, it was wide open. That would do the trick.

Johnny, carrying a thin black book, came running back so swiftly he was practically upon them before Frank noticed him. This time of day he was usually away. Now he stood beside Ben, opened his book and began reading. None of them spoke, understanding not a word, except Ben. He took the little chap's brown hand in his. It all took about a minute, and Johnny emerged from the tent.

He and Frank exchanged gestures. Johnny put a finger to his forehead, his expression puckered. Frank knew what he meant. That word *Kaddish* had been his clue. Had Ben not lost his sight the two might have communicated through their eyes. They might have recognised each other, or at least suspected that they had something in common.

Wally was heard from inside the tent, a gentler voice. 'Well, well', he said, 'Ben's little Wog padre.'

Frank caught himself swallowing hard. He was suddenly ashamed of the way some Australians had turned the place over when they captured Benghazi.

7 · *The Little Woman and the Great Big Army*

Heart pounding, she presented herself at the recruiting office of the women's army early in March 1942, intent upon breaking a promise she had faithfully made her husband. He had implored her to take any work rather than join up while he was abroad. As a married woman, she had no obligation towards national service. Indeed, only three months had passed since, to the misgiving of a large part of the population, even single women became liable for the call-up. One member of parliament had declared in a debate preceding the measure: 'The ATS (Auxiliary Territorial Service) has a thoroughly bad reputation. The condition of the camps is bad, the physical condition of some of the girls is bad, and the whole service has a bad name. . . . There is a general impression that the ATS is not the sort of service that a nice girl goes into.' According to another member: 'We are the first civilised country to propose that women should be drafted. The Nazis tried it and failed.'

Those MPs made a strong case. A women's service had been stitched haphazardly together only two years previous to the outbreak of war, and thoroughly deserved its reputation as an unnecessary shambles. It was officered by daughters of the gentry without managerial experience, or experience of any kind that did not come within the activities of what the newspapers then described as 'society'. The other ranks largely comprised young women desperate to escape from a constricted home life. Many of the girls had run away to enlist against their families' wishes. With the war, and the half-hearted application of military discipline to the ATS, the situation deteriorated. Some girls deserted, some deliberately got themselves pregnant to secure discharge under the notorious 'Paragraph Eleven', while others cracked beneath the regimental strain and had to be collected by their relatives or hospitalised.

Worst of all, the military authorities refused to take the ATS seriously, often keeping the units idle in their quarters and at the very best relegating them to the meanest tasks. Male soldiers were under no illusion as to the women's true function, describing them as 'officers' groundsheets'. No married soldier in his right senses would consent to his wife's voluntary enrolment.

Sylvia Litvinoff had not forewarned her husband, and on intimating her decision to don khaki to her mother and mother-in-law, she encountered discouragement in the strongest terms from both. She had now been a grass widow for ten months, and had received only half a dozen letters from the Middle East. Because of the military censorship, the letters told very little about her man's life out there, with no indication of course as to his actual whereabouts. She had taken work in London, but the passivity of the home routine filled her with impatience and discontent.

Sylvia's family had passed a rough decade in Dublin, by which time Alec Roytman bowed to his daughters' pressure to return to London. Why not open a new chapter in his somewhat stumbling career in the furniture industry? Had the decision been Alec's alone, he might well have allowed them all to linger out an existence beside the Liffey, himself resigning, with the aid of an occasional brandy, from the struggle to get himself established as a respectable businessman.

Alec's two eldest daughters were now accustomed to driving the engine. Anne and Sylvia had never accepted Dublin, from their point of view a poor specimen of a European city. They were the family's only consistent bread-winners. Alec possessed a skill rare in the Irish Free State that followed the partition of 1921. He could sell all the furniture he could make, and more, had his character equalled his expertise. Unhappily, he was eternally in debt to the timber merchant, the saw mill and, ultimately, the landlord of his workshop as well as his home. If he earned a few pounds, he could not be trusted to bring the money back reasonably intact.

Alec had no problem paying his workers, for there were just two – his eldest sons, for whom he did not regard wages as appropriate. In fact, when the two girls, in their late teens, declared it was time to bid the Emerald Isle farewell, one of the sons had slammed the door behind him and married a Catholic. This, in the eyes of the Dublin Jewish community, was a greater crime than robbing a bank, and a catastrophe tantamount to the destruction of the Temple in Jerusalem.

The girls insisted upon returning to London because employment other than domestic service or unskilled factory labour was hardly available in Dublin to working-class women without reasonable education. Virtually the sole substantial employer of women, the Irish Hospital Sweepstake Trust, was where they spent their days, and often their evenings too. The family could make good use of their overtime extras. Theirs was work of enormous concentration, operating primitive punch-card machines (forerunner of the computer) at speed, the holes corresponding to lucky numbers attached to runners in the Epsom Derby. Until the football pools era properly arrived, the Irish Sweep served the speculative instincts of the masses as an alternative to betting on horses and greyhounds.

The decision made, Sylvia was deputed in 1936 to travel to London with a younger sister as advance party. On learning of it, Rosa Levy, to the wonderment of her four Litvinoff sons, invited the two girls provisionally to lodge with us. Rosa, with a score of nine, was at last beyond child-bearing age. We rented a house that had seen better times, but accommodated us sufficiently well to give temporary shelter to visitors in the 'parlour'. No further need to delve than to state that Sylvia's arrival sent a frisson through the Litvinoff ranks, three of whom were now out of their teens, with myself, aged 18, a junior clerk in the gas company and the only one with a permanent job.

It confused us that she brought a tennis racket, a game for snobs and cissies. Sylvia informed us of her membership of a Jewish social club and her favourite recreations: dancing and country rambles. We stole furtive glances at her when she applied lipstick, and enjoyed a good laugh behind her back. We shared absolutely no experience of girls in this home where the children had grown up against a background of fashion talk. Sex was a taboo subject. The Litvinoff boys spent their leisure camping, cycling and attending political demonstrations, mainly those organised by the East London Communist Party.

The first Monday morning of Sylvia's stay gave us our greatest occasion for mirth. Waving a slip of paper she declared she was going to 'this address' to get a job. We found the statement hilarious. If there was a subject in which we claimed expert knowledge it was the job market. My brothers were in and out of work all the time, a condition regarded as absolutely normal to the lower orders in the 1930s. At that precise moment nearly three million of them were unemployed. Sylvia would learn. We gave her instructions as to where to board the 38 bus, which would take her to a newish office block in Holborn. It was a place we knew well from the outside as a convenient staging-post in the regular cycle run to Hyde Park and our free entertainment as hecklers at Speakers' Corner.

Sylvia returned about noon the same day. We were stupefied. Yes, she had the job and was promised one also for her elder sister Anne on her arrival the following week. Surely there must be some mistake! What kind of machines did she say they operated? Obviously not a typewriter, since Sylvia confessed her inability to type. The tiny holes she made in the punch cards stored information that could be retrieved by working another machine. Other companies besides the Irish Sweepstake authorities used them. Truly, it mystified us.

Among the differences, manifestly, that separated man from

woman loomed this subject of work. Women looked upon employment as their normal situation. Many men saw it as abnormal, signing on at the labour exchange being more natural to them. Moreover, when Anne arrived from Dublin, the two girls went off and found a little flat almost with the same speed and ease as securing employment. They had no reason to consult their parents first. The girls immediately set about purchasing lampshades and furnishings for their new home, cheerfully signing the credit forms. Their parents could not understand an English document anyway.

Sylvia and Anne travelled to their office together and returned together, as far as we could discern never a cross word exchanged. They hummed the music of Ivor Novello and arias from *Madame Butterfly*. The contrasts between the two families extended to their distinctive attitudes to life as a whole. The Roytmans, being mainly female, thought of life as something to enjoy; ours, emphatically male except for mother and one little sister, saw it as having to be endured. We were a house divided, theirs a united home. On the day I volunteered to show Sylvia our local greenery, Hackney Downs, it was the first time I had walked along the street with a female outside my own family circle.

When I spoke, she listened without interruption, confusing my smattering of education with maturity. Yet she had read more classical writers than I, and related the plots of such novelists as H. De Vere Stacpoole and Michael Arlen that no Litvinoff would touch with a poker held in a gloved hand. Until I explained the expressions, Sylvia had not heard that capitalism and communism were opposing doctrines, or that a document called the Balfour Declaration had brought the Jews streaming back to Palestine. Her own schooling had ceased when her father found a job for her, not yet fourteen, as messenger girl in a Dublin dress shop.

Well before I had left the gas company in 1938, Sylvia had progressed to an administrative position at the *Daily Sketch* newspaper, bringing home a salary substantially above that of the average working man. She resigned in December 1940, when we married in the interval between two air raids and had five months together prior to my departure on the *Orduña* for the Middle East. Her marriage to the youngest Litvinoff created some consternation in his family. Surely he was not yet old enough to know his own mind! However, they observed the desolation Sylvia suffered at our separation and all was graciously forgiven.

Unknown to me, she had constructed a strategy by which we were to be reunited, even in the teeth of the miserable war news. With matters left to Mr Churchill, the succession of defeats could easily take years out of one's life. Sylvia intended to attach conditions to her proposal to volunteer for the ATS. In the first place, she would demand to be trained as an army driver so as to be mobile rather than shunted into a desk job, or perhaps fall into the ignominy of some Aldershot kitchen. She could no longer tolerate remaining in one place while a world war swirled about her. Then she would insist upon a posting to the Middle East, for that was where she would encounter her Barney, with luck for regular weekends. The Middle East Command extended in those days from Cyprus in the north to Abyssinia and Somaliland in the south, and from Libya stretching far into Iraq, about 2,000 miles in any direction across three continents. Hence she needed to be a driver in charge of her own vehicle. Among the lacunae in Sylvia's education geography featured prominently. The Middle East Command, as she then conjectured it, might have occupied a space no more extensive than the county of Essex.

Her interview at the recruiting office, the first move in her plan for speedy reunion with her husband, war or no war, did not proceed as she had anticipated. She had visualised a warm welcome to the ranks, then a crammer's course on the internal combustion engine and prompt departure for warmer climes. They explained that volunteering was the patriotic thing to do, especially since the ATS was desperately short of personnel. Unhappily, she was ineligible to qualify as a driver since her height, five feet, left her four inches below the minimum. She must be processed through in the usual way, and in whatever branch deemed necessary by the 'higher ups'. As to a posting to the Middle East, that was beyond anyone's power to grant. This war sent His Majesty's Forces to all parts of the world, women soldiers too. But no specific requirements could be entertained.

Somewhat disenchanted, Sylvia departed without signing on the dotted line. Her husband had enlightened her enough about the army to convince her that once it had you in its clutches you were its chattel, to be blown in the wind like a fallen leaf. She consequently wrote a formal letter of application, addressed to the head of the service at the War Office, and again stipulated her conditions for enrolment. This was early in 1942, when the ATS still suffered from its non-attraction as a service for a nice girl. Quickly she received a reply to the effect that her desire to become a driver with an eventual posting to the Middle East Command would, as far as circumstances allowed, be honoured. There was an address near Kings Cross where she could enlist. It was no more than she expected.

Furnished with a travel pass and four shillings on account of her first week's pay, she boarded a crowded train with a chorus of other female recruits. After a six-hour journey in an unheated compartment and no possibility to obtain refreshment, they arrived at the ATS base camp at Glencorse, near Edinburgh. Still in civilian clothes, they all took careful steps in their high heels and were distributed to various hutments. The first parade the next day proved slightly traumatic: the camp barber unceremoniously sheared off their long hair. Some of the girls wept.

What next? Imploring forgiveness, Sylvia wrote to her husband almost daily, long letters that told of her relief at shaking free from the bleak London round. Real living since his departure had expired in pointless drudgery at temporary work during the day, and many evenings and nights spent in the 'Anderson' shelter at the bottom of the garden while the bombs dropped. This, and the national recreation of the deserted wife: knitting sweaters and scarves for a distant husband. It merits recollection that the period brought letter-writing to a level of activity without parallel in Britain before or since. My mother, too, applied herself to conquering the language sufficiently to keep in touch with her sons at war.

The training camp proved, even to more worldly women than Sylvia, a chastening experience. The ATS rankers found the discipline, taken to farcical lengths, irksome. They could not fully accustom themselves to a system that denied direct speech with a commissioned officer, only via a corporal or sergeant. Such were 'normal channels'. And the end of privacy. It was all one to Sylvia, since her programme was pre-determined: to follow this comedy with her driving instruction and an early posting to that Promised Land called the Middle East. She felt no inclination to offer her husband a run-down of how she became transformed into a soldier – not a word even of the influenza that swept through the Scottish camp and laid her low for a couple of weeks.

In one of her letters she wrote:

My beloved Barney, my search for peace and quiet has led me to the only tranquil corner in the whole of this benighted place, the 'quiet room' of the YM, though even here the babble insists on following me through the double doors. I have just had a lovely long talk with Fanny [another younger sister in the army] over the phone – she exploits her position on the telephone exchange to the full – and wished her many happy returns of the morrow. Twenty-two tomorrow, and she complains of feeling woefully ancient. God, the tragedy of it! To be young and have no time for youth. Just look at the youngsters in your family and mine, all of them slogging away, their lives overshadowed by the atmosphere in which they must live, their minds never freed for one moment from the overhanging clouds of present fears and future anxieties!

. . . And what of us, and the thousands like us? Every precious moment slipping away, moments of which we have been cheated while the fever of war still stretches over the globe. If only I could smile and be frivolous like you! To

The Little Woman and the Great Big Army

me our parting is a pain that is as much part of me as your spirit which possesses me so completely. . . . I can't believe that almost a year has passed since that fateful day in May when we separated. Somehow I can't define this 'parting' in any measure of *time*. Time has failed to dim the memory of our heavenly interlude.

. . . Last night I went to the flicks to see Alice Faye warble through some exotic film called *Weekend in Havana*, and oh, the painfully sweet recollection of my Barney, clumping up the stairs in his army boots and unmelodiously singing that song, *You say the sweetest things, baby, you've got me riding high*. I felt you were there. Ridiculous, don't you think that Alice Faye has the power to make me hunger for you?

. . . My training here is finished, and thank God. It was tough while it lasted. We shan't know where they are sending us yet. Girls I know have had grand luck in their postings, billeted in quite luxurious surroundings and doing the most interesting work while others have fared badly. . . . I have many friends here, even though we belong to the 'common herd'. And that's a good sign. However, until they understand how it is I can refrain from smoking, swearing and visiting the local pubs they will continue to be puzzled by me. They find lots of opportunities to flirt with any bombardier in the neighbourhood.

. . . No, Barney, despite my horrific initiation into this life I could not go back – or want to go back – to home and friends, comfort and books and music, unless you were there to share it all. . . . So glad you found some use for the 'winter' pullover. The white shirt was included purely to please my artistic sense. In any case, it occurred to me it might help to keep you cool.

. . . I was regaled this week with a most welcome parcel from your mum containing a gorgeous cake and, among other delicacies, those rare things, tomatoes. There was a grand letter too, written in her usual painstaking way, giving me all the news from the home front. I am so glad to tell you that she has heard from brother Pinny, so that our fears for his whereabouts were unfounded. He is well, and hoping to come across you somewhere in the East.

I never received this or any other letter despatched during many months in 1942. Eventually they all returned to their senders stamped with the formula: 'It is regretted that this item could not be delivered because the addressee is reported prisoner of war.'

Her group was posted to a women's transport unit near Hereford, and placed in the tender care of a cockney sergeant who could twirl a grease-gun round his little finger, and many of the girls too. Sergeant Morris had inherited the style of command favoured during the previous war. He bullied the novices, insulted their intelligence, kept them down on their knees changing wheels till they could fix them in their sleep. Detecting the ghost of a superior attitude in Sylvia, Morris tried all the usual army tricks to break her spirit: separating her from the rest to clean up the garage, then the barrack room. The man believed a transport company was no place for a woman, and constantly told them so. He made Sylvia acquire various processes by heart and repeat them in front of the others, as in school, such as: The starter motor, sparking plugs, lights, horn and sometimes other items, all need electricity. This is made by a dynamo and is stored in a battery.

'Why don't you complain about the bastard to our own subaltern [the female lieutenant]?' her friends asked Sylvia. But she would not impair her strategy. Passing out successfully as a driver as soon as possible would bring her one step nearer her goal.

One day a notice pinned up in her barrack room stated that a Jewish chaplain would be visiting the camp the following Sunday. This would be a voluntary church parade for personnel of that faith. Those interested should make their way to the usual chaplain's hut at 10 am. It could be of interest, thought Sylvia, though she had experienced no great yearning for spiritual solace. At least, meeting other Jewish girls could give a savour of home. They would surely have things to talk about.

The Little Woman and the Great Big Army

The Hereford camp extended over a wide acreage, but at last she found the hut. It was empty. Ten minutes went by: no sign of the padre, nor anyone else. Impatiently, she stamped some warmth into her feet and glumly perused the posters decorating the hut. She was about to leave when the door opened. There, standing before her was the scowling face of Sgt Morris. For a moment he was stunned. So was she.

When he found his voice it was plaintive, quite other than the one he customarily employed. He flung his arms outward, Al Jolson style. 'Why didn't yer te-e-ell me?' he said. Thenceforward Sylvia had no trouble at Hereford, he was a lamb towards her. She duly passed with flying colours, hugging a precious identification card called A.2038. Signed by the Permanent Under Secretary of State for War, this stated that the undersigned, ATS W/135305 Sylvia Litvinoff, height five feet, eyes grey, hair brown, being employed on Military Service, is hereby authorised by the Secretary of State for War to drive a motor car, lorry, motor cycle or other mechanically propelled vehicle when on Government duty. A proud moment!

She wrote enthusiastically: 'Darling, last weekend was thrilling in that I went on my first real convoy, and it was exciting. About 50 vehicles of varying sizes took off (I was assigned one of the heaviest) and we drove to an RAF depot where men of the camp and Fleet Air Arm loaded the lorries with aeroplane parts. These we had to deliver to a camp over a hundred miles away. We arrived in excellent order, unloaded and were made a great fuss of by our fellows in blue. We stayed there overnight and travelled back the next day without mishap. A grand and enjoyable experience.' Another letter never received.

They sent her to an ordnance depot in the northern suburbs of London, where she found herself the sole woman among 17 men. Cosy as that sounded, in practice Sylvia was compelled to run the gauntlet of their constant sarcasm and broad humour. Crash the gears and the lot of them applauded derisively. Each time she applied at the stores for a piece of equipment it was greeted by guffaws, for there appeared no limit to the sexual *double entendre* it might evoke. But she was billeted with a solicitous old couple in their house and, happily, could dash home on an evening or weekend and keep closely in touch with both her families. More, she was awarded a stripe as lance-corporal (an extra sixpence a day) and given sole command of a small 'utility' truck to carry despatches all over the Home Counties. She came to know the blacked-out, bomb-scarred city like a veteran taxi-driver. Everything was proceeding as she wished. One day Sylvia intimated to her circle in Hackney that her name had gone forward for a commission to officer rank. However, as summer drew on no word arrived from her husband, wherever he might be in the Middle East.

The dreaded news reached her in the impersonal language of a standardised letter in July 1942. Her eyes could see only the typewritten details. Private Litvinoff, RAMC, was posted as 'missing' on 28 May. Then the formula usual in such communications: 'The report that he is missing does not necessarily mean that he has been killed, as he may be a prisoner of war or temporarily separated from his regiment.'

The letter was placed in Sylvia's hands as, attired in dungarees, she was engaged on maintenance work on her vehicle. Numb, she knew she was not about to cry. She could not speak. She knew she had to be with her mother-in-law Rosa. By this time the two families had several members in the services — Rosa's four big sons, two of Sylvia's mother Rebecca's daughters. Only Barney belonged to them both. Her head ringing, Sylvia returned to her billet, changed into civilian clothes and caught a bus to Hackney. She forgot she was in the army.

Two black days, during which she could neither eat nor sleep, followed. Drifting from her home to his, avoiding any other contact, she worked her life back to their brief interlude together more than a year in the past, but a dream. A hundred 'if onlies' crossed her mind. She could have prevented his posting abroad, there were ways. She could be having his child, if only she had insisted when he wavered. She was now

26, he a year younger, if he lived. *If* he lived. . . . With the third day letters of sympathy began pouring in, sisters, relatives and friends begging her to keep hoping, and have patience. How had they learned?

She found reading the correspondence an effort. Mechanically, that afternoon, she dressed in her uniform again. Leaden feet took her back to the depot. It was as good a place as any to wait, probably the best place. Her company commander, a man, met her sympathetically. The entire depot had the news. But, he said, this was the army, with a war on its hands. No one could simply walk away. She was to accompany him to the 'old man' – the colonel in charge.

He too adopted a sympathetic line towards Sylvia. Colonel Justin Stone, a career soldier risen through the ranks and already in his forties, spoke to her like a father (not *her* father) and informed her she would not be punished this time. Surely she must realise that absence without leave from the important work of the depot constituted a most serious military offence? He rose, and placed a hand on her shoulder. 'Now, my dear, go back to your work. We shall all pray for you.'

Several weeks elapsed and another communication arrived for Sylvia, from the RAMC Records Department. The buff-coloured card, no larger than the label on a pot of jam, read: 'Should we not receive news of your husband within the next few weeks we regret he must be presumed killed and your married woman's allowance will therefore cease.' They were paying her 32 shillings and sixpence per week, in addition to her lance-corporal's pay of 16 shillings. She refrained from showing the card to her mother-in-law.

I was in fact held with a small group of medicals treating the wounded brought to Benghazi at the time. The situation in the desert had reached momentary stagnation. General Rommel's panzers had crossed the Egyptian frontier, where they prepared their final push to Cairo. Skirmishing in the El Alamein salient left the issue undecided, but British prisoners arriving in the Benghazi cage spoke of a forthcoming counter-attack. Benghazi was held by the Italians, who were evacuating prisoners fast. An Italian padre arrived to seek Medical Corps volunteers to stay behind to tend the wounded. Those doing so, the padre promised, could write a letter which he undertook to convey to the Vatican for onward transmission.

I leapt at the opportunity, not altogether from selfless motives. In Libya the possibility of rescue always existed; once in Italy I would be stuck, to live the war out in captivity. Moreover, the Mediterranean was also a war zone and could just as easily provide a grave as the desert. I remained behind and wrote my letter. Thanks to the Vatican, my family received news of my fate before the Red Cross or the War Office. Mercifully, Sylvia's married woman's allowance continued.

Her sole desire now was to avoid a posting outside the London area and retain the closest contact with home and news. Abandoning any idea of an officer's commission, she resolved to preserve the freedom her little vehicle granted, and perform her work as a despatch rider till the war ended or her husband returned home, whichever came first. Purpose returned to her actions. She could write again, and send parcels. All might end sooner than the depressing war news indicated.

Yes, news! Barney would want to know everything about the progress of the campaigns, the Russian front too, and that, she mistakenly presumed, would surely not be possible during his incarceration. She found an old exercise book belonging to her youngest sister – only a few pages used, in childish arithmetic – and began a diary, starting from the day of her husband's capture. Feverishly, she entered the main events of the war, notes of Churchill's speeches, anxieties over her mother's health, chit-chat about theatre and concerts attended, abbreviated notes on other items of family news, on the weather. This became a discipline to help the speeding of the days.

Unsuspected by Sylvia, Colonel Stone had been observing her from his office window at the depot. He was not alone in his interest. Highly visible as the only woman driver, she represented a focus of sorts for the instincts of men who, like herself, were desperately tired of the war, the *longueurs* following Allied defeats, the separation from loved ones. Much to her surprise, she became the recipient of confidences, not least from a red-cheeked, heavy-drinking sergeant-major feared by all, and from an erudite corporal who passed her notes containing mysterious phrases she could not understand, for they were in Latin. Three years of personal disarray had wrought havoc with natural masculine reserve. Everyone felt frustrated, lonely and in need of a Wailing Wall.

One morning Sylvia was summoned to appear before the colonel. 'Corporal Litvinoff, your duties are changed', he informed her. 'I am taking you as my staff driver.' Shocked at the thought that this would put a stop to her freedom of movement, she vehemently protested. She didn't want a job that entailed waiting at the wheel while he attended meetings and those social occasions officers always appeared to have plenty of time for. She pictured herself out in the cold on a country road somewhere in England as he whiled hours away in a pub with some colonel crony.

'Besides, Sir', she told him. 'I shan't be able to manage it. Your car is a large Humber and I won't see over the bonnet or reach the controls. I do want to stay in my present job.'

'The car will be adjusted. The mechanics are attending to it. Report tomorrow morning.' In this depot, obscurely tucked behind the North Circular Road, Colonel Stone was the Great Dictator.

Sylvia was furious. And naive. The entire depot construed the situation to confirm their inevitable suspicions. The poor woman's husband was out of reach. Some of them knew the colonel's lady, not a great beauty, rather timid, a typically apprehensive, dutiful appendage to the military apparatus. Not uncommonly, it fell to such women to await a husband's attention in a succession of stations, never a proper home, as he pompously ruled in the officers' mess. Stone was an honourable man, no one disputed it, but this was wartime after all. 'Shouldn't be surprised if she wangled the job herself', one of her comrades was heard to remark about Sylvia.

Meanwhile the war news improved, and she received

regular letters, every three or four weeks, from her husband, now detained in Italy. Her hopes reached a peak when, in July 1943, Mussolini was overthrown and Italy capitulated. He must soon be home! Urgently she bought him a typewriter and took his one good civilian suit to be valeted. Vacant flats were virtually non-existent in London at that time, or became available only against a premium quite beyond her capacity. She began looking none the less, and put her name down with the housing department of the borough council. 'How would you like to live in Hampstead?' she wrote. 'It's my favourite district.' Hampstead meant nothing to me, except for its fair on bank holidays. 'Mummy says she will get some money from Daddy and buy us furniture.' Poor Sylvia! We had now been apart for over two years and she was dreaming castles in the air. In September she forced herself to realise that our reunion lay still in the distant future, for she learnt that I had been whisked away to Silesia, on the Polish border.

Despite her earlier reservations, driving Colonel Stone about his business made her days tolerable. He called her Sylvia, and she appreciated his interest in her affairs, never failing to enquire about her mother's health, which was critical, and news of her husband. He expressed curiosity regarding her Jewish religion and Russian name. Where did her people originate? It apparently impressed him when she described me as a writer. En route to a meeting on the other side of London one day Stone invited her to join him for a drink at Verrey's bar, a favourite haunt of the élite in Regent Street. A trifle self-consciously, he asked her please to call him Justin when away from the depot. What was going on in his mind became obvious to her, but she had grown to like the colonel and enjoyed his wry conversation. She once asked, impulsively, 'Would you care to meet my mother? It will only be a short detour on the way back to the depot.'

'I'd like that', he replied. She brought the stiff Englishman to her Hackney dwelling, introducing him to this elderly, plump woman who tortured his language. They had tea. Justin met the two youngest girls of the family. He was courtesy itself. On the return journey he opened up. 'Cissy can't have children', he disclosed. 'She's not happy, and nor am I. How we'll get on after this lot ends and I get my bowler hat I really don't know. I can't bear the prospect, actually.'

She drove in silence. It required all her skill to steer the Humber through those darkened back streets. But on another journey he told her: 'Your Barney isn't likely to come home, Sylvia dear. The Germans are doing frightful things to the Jews. Marry me, and I'll convert. I've never been much of a Christian anyway. I love you.'

None of this went into her diary, though in July 1943 she had made an entry: 'Began working on Overlord with J.S.' Several years would pass before it emerged that Sylvia was among the earliest to be given the code-word for the Allied assault upon Europe. (Eleven months were still to elapse before that great day in 1944.) There was a secretive side to her nature anyway, and not for a moment did she detect that she and her colonel were the gossip of the depot. Cissie set his junior officers on the task of keeping her informed. Sylvia had no idea of it. They could learn little anyway. Barney's arrival home was where her thoughts lingered. Her mother, in hospital for suspected cancer, gave cause for the greatest anxiety.

The months ground out their tormenting course. In January 1945, she told her diary: 'Feel we are at our lowest ebb since Dunkirk. Germans fighting strongly in Belgium, in the Vosges and at Budapest. In spite of the appointment of a Regent for Greece and formation of a new government the fighting continues in Athens. And last night, too, the rockets and bombs were shattering. To Barney I wrote gleefully that I had seen and decided to take the flat in Acton. What a sorry mess it all is! Took mummy to the hospital. Our hopes were crushed for they confirmed she has a growth and must return for radium treatment. And I could only write to Barney about the flat.'

It suddenly came to her that she hated the army and needed to be rid of it. From time to time she received compassionate leave to manage the home during Rebecca's absence, which mainly entailed coping with her increasingly difficult father.

A Very British Subject

Additionally, she wanted desperately to spend time with her husband's mother Rosa, suffering together with her.

Meanwhile, the colonel was not ready to surrender. She appreciated his friendship and worried for his Cissie, as revealed in another of her diary entries. 'Justin returned from Torquay. Hope all is well now with him and his wife.'

All was not well, so much was painfully evident. Justin continued to telephone Sylvia at home during her periods of leave, seeking a meeting. On about the third refusal, he abjectly resorted to the ultimate banality, announcing to her that he was about to commit suicide. Sylvia took him at his empty word. She rushed to her mother, released from hospital a few days earlier. 'Justin said he is going to commit suicide, Mummy!', she cried. 'What shall I do?' Sensible Rebecca remained unmoved. 'They never do, Sylvie, when they tell you first.'

We met, the four of us, when at last I returned, thankfully in good health, after four years' absence from England. Justin invited Sylvia and her reclaimed husband to dinner at the Cumberland Hotel, and there was music. As I danced with Cissie she admitted all to me. 'It was just a passing phase, Barney', she whispered. 'I'm sure he's getting over it.'

Had the army and our separation changed Sylvia? Certainly she had lost weight, but none of her radiance. The little Dubliner now smoked. Her capacity to expel the army experience totally from her mind astonished me. Were it not for some photographs in uniform, no outsider could have suspected it. Like all the ATS she received 56 clothing coupons on her demobilisation, then deliberately stripped herself of every military memory. Forty years on I learned of the existence of that diary scrawled into her little sister's school book. It lay unread and forgotten, by Sylvia herself, in a trunk filled with ancient letters and sundry wartime papers.

Rosa paid a mother's penalty for the long war. She saw all her sons return safely home, then died early in 1947, still a young woman. Rebecca, despite her chronic poor health, enjoyed another 20 years.

8 · A.W.O.L.

Victory in Europe was accorded a day of celebration on 8 May 1945, throughout the English-speaking world, but I could have no part of it. I was still awaiting repatriation to England from my last German prison camp in Memmingen, Bavaria.

When finally the Emperor Hirohito authorised the Japanese government to sign surrender terms three more months had elapsed. By this time I had returned to England, still a private soldier and languishing in the heart of Devon. The British army seemed peculiarly addicted to the principle that husbands and wives, sons and mothers, should be kept as far apart as Britain's physical extent would allow. Following some weeks of leave granted me as an ex-prisoner they had sent me up to Yorkshire, after which I was posted to a military camp outside Newton Abbot. That's where Hirohito's authorisation found me, separated by over 200 miles from everything I held dear in London.

This did not arise from my importance to the security of the realm. Both in Yorkshire and Devon I performed immensely pointless tasks invented by the generals to keep their army out of mischief. By some ordinance, accepted without question, I was reserved for the implementation of military tidiness and hygiene. In Yorkshire I was restricted to cleaning the barrack floors. In Devon I was deprived of the company of my family, and the jollification envisioned as appropriate to victory against Japan, by the urgency of ensuring that our camp paths remained free of weeds. In this endeavour I was joined by Private Tony Lofting.

Prison years had brought me together with Lofty in all vicissitudes, though we had never considered ourselves close comrades. He and I reached England in the same aircraft, then to Yorkshire on the same train; now once again, and wielding a weapon no more lethal than a garden fork while the powers in the War Department leisurely pursued their obligation to return Britain's citizen army to the normal world. Millions of us were still awaiting release. At Newton Abbot, Lofty and I truly discovered each other as working-class Londoners marooned for no good reason among those unfortunate enough to originate in other parts of the United Kingdom. By right of birth we cockneys were superior to all, and in that dismissive sweep we included our camp commandant, who came from Ireland.

Lofty, a truly dependable companion in the science of passive resistance, faithfully adhered to the principle that the only reward for finishing a job quickly was to be given another. Good humoured under stress, he could be surly when it suited him. As former prisoners and veterans of the earliest campaigns we were hardened, and permitted a certain latitude – or so we flattered ourselves. In truth, we mostly acquiesced to discipline in uttermost docility, the result of stultifying years at the receiving end of orders that denied the use of all initiative. The strictest limits were incorporated in the elasticity of Section 40 of the Army Act, contained in a red booklet that served as the khaki Bible.

Like me, Lofty was a married man yearning to restore a domestic touch to his personal life. And here we were, killing one more afternoon whose morrow was declared to be VJ Day. 'We never got home for VE Day, and they expect us to spend VJ Day in this bleeding hole', Lofty complained.

'Just our luck', I agreed.

'Well then, why don't we piss off?'

'Without a travel warrant? How far do you expect to get before the redcaps pick us up?' A soldier buying his own railway ticket invariably aroused suspicion in those days, and we could never succeed in leaving camp in civilian clothes. Lofty threw a graphic gesture of impatience that involved some business with his backside.

A.W.O.L.

'Travel warrant!' he exclaimed, as if such treasure had less consequence than a discarded Woodbine packet. 'We'll go for the evening train to London. They'll be so busy at Newton Abbot station they'd wave us through the turn-stile on a sheet of toilet paper.'

In a wartime era when the efficient transportation of men and machines could decide the fate of nations, trains survived as dinosaurs lethargically roaming over Britain at a momentum all their own. From Devon they came within the gentle aegis of the Great Western Railway. Its staff of officials, who trusted themselves on no vehicle except the bicycle, were monarchs of all they surveyed – in this case yellowing maps covered with names in tiny print and a pattern of tea stains. Yet virtually the entire population was eternally on the move. No one could foretell times of arrival and departure, relying on faith, luck and an engine driver's sense of direction.

Lofty was right. A huge crowd excitedly invaded the platform at Newton Abbot while station personnel leaned away from the pressure. We boarded, took up positions in the corridor and pushed at the windows for air. A long day's journey through the night brought us to Paddington. There, Lofty and I separated with barely a glance exchanged (soldiers' partings were nothing if not casual) and by the sunrise I arrived at Hackney, where my wife Sylvia had at last procured a top floor room with kitchenette for one pound a week.

I cannot recall whether the merry-making reached carnival proportions on VJ Day in Hackney, but 36 hours quickly passed in a round of reunions with various family members. Three households, in descending order of affluence as you progressed up the stairs, shared our dwelling. The landlord occupied the ground floor, a couple with two children the next, and above them all ourselves at the summit. Late on the second day discretion warned me I had better return to camp. I would slink into the barracks late that night and appear on parade the next morning with no one the wiser, nor the country less secure, for this brief absence from my post.

A haversack already shouldered, a delicate moment of sweet

sorrow parted Sylvia and me and I turned to go. Just then we heard a tap on the door. Our downstairs neighbour, her face ashen, poked in her head.

'There are two policemen below, asking for your husband.' She revealed the news in a solemn whisper. 'I told them to wait.' The presence of police could only imply bad news in Hackney. In fact they had followed her up the stairs, apprehensive perhaps lest I was of the calibre who hid in cupboards or sprang through windows.

The policemen filled our room. 'We've instructions to take you in', the spokesman of the two informed me. 'Absent without leave.' I assured them I was returning to the army that very moment; obviously so, I was in uniform. No, they had their orders, so would I kindly accompany them without resistance.

That night I spent locked in the solitary cell housed in the Dalston police station, a building often passed in earlier days, though never penetrated. By the standards of the time the accommodation proved not uncomfortable. I slept well, and received a wholesome breakfast next morning while expecting the full weight of the law to come crushing down upon me. Nothing happened for several hours, until two redcaps appeared and took me by car to Scotland Yard, then situated on the Embankment by Whitehall. The Corps of Military Police held a lease on a section of that forbidding edifice, where doubtless retribution for every offence from drunkenness to cowardice in the face of the enemy could be summarily dispensed. Not too summarily, as it happened, in my case.

One might reasonably surmise that a British soldier's worst moments of his life would ensue from confrontation with a superior foe in battle. Not so. He dreaded the military police even more. We regarded the redcaps as our principal enemy. According to legend, they took you in at the least provocation, subjected you to physical violence, broke your spirit and discarded you only when they deemed you were rendered invertebrate. Stories were legion of how they conducted their notorious 'glasshouse' at Shepton Mallet. Apparently every horror in the catalogue of inhumanity was perpetrated there – deprivation of food, cold water torture, pack-drill until you dropped. Moreover, it was not wholly legend. Terrified, I surrendered to the officer in charge for interrogation at Scotland Yard.

He was the mildest, most youthful army officer I had ever encountered, perhaps 19 years of age, bespectacled, and it seemed more afraid of me than I of him. One could visualise such a person at his most brutal in a Sixth Form chess tournament. The man evinced no interest in my alleged misdeed. On the contrary, he sought reassurance as to my health and general welfare. Was I under treatment for any sickness? Had I any complaints to register regarding my arrest? Married or single? Did I wish to speak to an ordained clergyman? There was a C. of E. padre in attendance and those of other faiths were readily available. No, none of these. He had nothing more to add, save that an escort was due from my unit to return me to my place of service. A redcap corporal marched me down below.

All possessions, including money, keys, wrist-watch and shaving-kit were delivered to him, everything in fact except a book I had packed to lighten the journey back to Newton Abbot. After a search for cigarettes (none), I had to strip and walk through shallow water contained in a long, wide vessel, presumably a footbath. The ritual concluded with the restoration of my clothes, minus boots, and deposition in a cell all to myself. This surprised me, for I was by no means alone undergoing incarceration that day. Trafalgar Square, minutes away, could always guarantee a rich harvest for military police on the look-out for miscreants, who virtually formed a queue awaiting arrest.

The cell was completely bare, without a chair or wash basin, and I stretched out morosely on the bedstead. But with my book (I had resolved to catch up with my education and it was Bertrand Russell's *Marriage and Morals*, to this day unfinished), I proposed to pass the time productively pending early release. A plate of food periodically brought to the cell door functioned as hour glass the following day, which began with a wash in cold water from an enamel basin.

Suddenly one of my jailors, a tall redcap, unlocked the door and entered. 'You all right, son?' he asked. This army had already stolen nearly six years of my life together with much of my élan and I was 27 years of age. 'I'm all right', I replied.

'What you got there? Hm, a book.' Without favouring the title with a glance he handled it. 'That'll be worth a bob or two at Foyle's. I'll give you a fag for it, and a light.' I wasn't going to have any of that. 'Don't smoke', I lied. The guard shrugged and left. It was to be assumed that everybody had his racket in this existence, and a shilling was still money in 1945. But the vision of this sturdy military policeman humping his plunder of books to Foyle's second-hand department at a bob a time struck me as pitiful inauguration of a career on the black market. Later, the young officer came on his rounds, to hear complaints. I had nothing to tell him. You didn't sneak on a prison guard into whose tender mercies you were entrusted.

They were busy the following day. I heard scuffles, roars of anger, an Irish song – the usual prisoners' chorus when soldiers were rounded up protesting innocence or acting defiantly abusive. Silence then reigned while the business associated with detention proceeded. I was pondering my fate when a hissing sound kept repeating from round the floor of my cell. I thought of an invasion of rodents. Did they hiss? Investigation produced an interesting discovery. The wall separating my cell from the one adjacent did not fit close to the ground, but left a gap of some two inches. The hissing emanated from the prisoner next door. I acknowledged it to be a greeting, and responded with a friendly 'Hello, there!'

'Hey, mate, you got a cigarette butt?' There was no mistaking the Glasgow brogue. He must have been desperate, the voice resonating with urgency.

'Sorry, no.'

'Turn out the lining of your pockets, and see if any baccy comes out of the seams.'

A.W.O.L.

'I never carry cigarettes.' It was a cruel statement of my position, conveyed to a man evidently in extremis. I awaited some reaction from the other side to learn to what depths I had goaded the poor wretch: suicide perhaps, madness at the very least. While a POW in Italy I had observed a sergeant starving himself as he traded his daily ration of bread, the size of a tennis ball, in exchange for the local 'Popolare' cigarettes. The brand, issued to prisoners in packets of five every few days, might have been contrived out of used tea-leaves.

What now? A gun shot perhaps. If a redcap proffered a cigarette in exchange for a book, there was no telling what higher transaction could emerge from something really valuable, maybe a gold watch or a diamond signet ring. My imagination zigzagged over grotesque possibilities. But there was no gun shot, nor the banging of a lunatic head against a wall – just silence. It could be a quiet case of suicide. I settled down to another night of uneasy sleep.

It was already my third morning in the cells when a general clearance took place with escorts arriving from all corners to collect. My neighbour now revealed himself as a diminutive squaddie of the Cameronians. He had managed to survive the night without a cigarette, or injury self-inflicted, and departed without so much as a nod to me in recognition of our brief interlocution at ground level.

The call rang out for Private Litvinoff. The inevitable corporal, with private soldier in support, took me under charge with no more formality than could be expected had I been a sack of potatoes: two youngsters, both strange to London. I knew them well from other times, when they would speak nostalgically of their home towns in the north of England and I hinted, without a grain of truth, at escapades involving the fast life in the big city. I offered them a smile radiating welcome, good to see you – a sentiment genuinely felt, at least in part.

But they were transformed, those two. Hitherto we had been lads together, enjoying a joke or a gripe as circumstances pre-scribed. Now, however, the relationship was altered. They embodied authority, I the criminal fraternity. According to our regimental code they did not carry arms but presented a spruced-up appearance, web gaiters and belt well blancoed, the quintessence of officialdom. I did most of the talking.

'Before taking the train back, I would consider it a favour if you'd allow me to say goodbye to my mother. It won't take long. How about it?' My pleading softened the corporal's heart. 'Where does she live?', he asked.

'In Hackney. We can pick up the bus in Shaftesbury Avenue.' Realising that neither of them had the faintest idea where Hackney was situated, and conceivably had never heard of Shaftesbury Avenue (what did the average Englishman know of England beyond his own backyard in 1945?), I led them to the bus-stop. London's traffic had not yet gridlocked into its subsequent paralysis, and in twenty minutes we were at my mother's front door.

She evinced no surprise at my sudden appearance, nor at my condition as a soldier under arrest, and beckoned us in. Having lived through a mother's long nightmare when all her elder sons were away on military service, Rosa had trembled with every arrival of the post. All were back in England now, since when nothing unforeseen that befell them caused her anxiety or bewilderment. Quite composed, she enquired whether we had time for a cup of tea. I said: 'Yes please, Mum', while my escort nodded stiffly. Perhaps it came as a shock to them that their comrade's mother spoke in a foreign accent.

'We must leave now.' The corporal made an important pronouncement of it as he put down his cup. Once in the street, I perceived the two's perplexity at how to proceed to reach Paddington station. They gazed up and down the nondescript thoroughfare as though floundering in a maze.

Truth to tell, I wasn't absolutely sure myself, having travelled to my neighbourhood six dawns earlier in a taxi. A cockney born and bred, my life in this city had not been wide-ranging or adventurous. The exigencies of war had marshalled me over Britain entire, then to South Africa, Egypt, Cyprus, Iraq and other countries of the Middle East before fate visited me in Libya. Thereupon the enemy had transported me in the hold of a ship through the Corinth Canal into Italy, and thence by sealed train through Germany into Poland. I had resided in France previously as a civilian and knew, or thought I knew, that fair country. Characteristic of my working-class youth, I was acquainted with Leicester Square's cinemas. Additionally, I had patronised a Lyons Corner House, stood in Hyde Park to hear the speakers and camped in Epping Forest. This roughly comprised my knowledge of London remote from the East End, my range of exploration and curiosity having limited itself to what could be achieved on an afternoon's bicycle ride. But I would have been ashamed to admit such ignorance of a native city to these fellows from England's outer space.

'First on the 38 bus, then the tube', I announced. 'Of course, so let's get on with it', replied the corporal abruptly. However, intimately as I knew the Paris Métro, the London Underground, far more complicated, remained a somewhat closed book. Obviously my escort party knew it not at all. So I pretended to bring them to Paddington by the shortest route, a classic case of the halt leading the blind. My own neighbourhood was not then served by the Underground. The Victoria and Jubilee lines did not as yet exist, while the Central line gave out at Broad Street as if Bethnal Green and the route to Leytonstone constituted uninhabited swamplands still awaiting colonisation.

After reaching Piccadilly by the bus, we accepted the challenge of the tube. Affecting a seasoned experience of the meanderings of the London transport system, I refrained from consulting the helpful diagrams provided. Piccadilly Circus offered two alternatives, and I chose the one marked Gloucester Road. They did not demur. The line travelled in a westerly direction. I therefore surmised it could take us within Paddington's magnetic field. My own sense of assurance impressed me, and perhaps my companions too.

We flashed past Green Park and South Kensington within minutes, whereupon I noticed that beyond Gloucester Road the line continued through unknown subterranean territory beckoning the traveller into the wilds of Middlesex. I was now absolutely in charge.

'We change here', I stated. Jumping out at Gloucester Road, the others barely had time to follow before the doors closed upon them. Paddington was revealed on a sign listing stations covered by the Circle line. We sped along the platform, scurried down a stairway and to my relief caught a train just about to leave. It took a little time for me to realise we were moving in the wrong direction. Were our destination Victoria, we could not have been better placed.

A considerable period had now been spent in the tunnels excavated from London's clay, an hour at least. A quick, courageous decision was required and, outwardly relaxed, I stood and hung upon a strap until arriving at Victoria. There, we were enveloped by a phalanx of bodies pouring from the great terminus. My guardians shouldered up beside me as though anticipating their prisoner's sudden getaway. 'Another change', I called, and we leapt out.

All that was now required involved crossing over to the opposite platform. To do so by the shortest route would have exposed my ignorance. Consequently I led my companions out into the busy terminus proper, walked them round the exit so as to re-enter by another aperture that afforded a change of atmosphere, perspective and scene. Somewhat breathless, we thus returned to the Circle line and soon I was thankfully checking off the station signs in their correct order – Notting Hill Gate and Bayswater flowed past and Paddington loomed ahead. We had made it. The corporal uttered not a word as we alighted. His deputy had not spoken since we left Scotland Yard and did not choose this moment to break his silence. I experienced the gratification of a pilgrim arriving at Mecca. A responsibility lifted from my shoulders as I put myself back into their hands. Paddington signified the restoration of absolute military authority.

Tony Lofting and I were reunited at camp for judgement to be pronounced in fulfilment of the law. An entire week separated our illicit departure from our enforced return. Not

A.W.O.L.

too much fuss here, the offence merited a longish period confined to barracks. Lofty and I accepted the punishment as a technical victory, for what was there worth doing on a free evening in Newton Abbot? Surely a pleasant enough market town, and the cider was good, but the place barely contained any real distractions for us sophisticated men from London.

While we were kept within the camp's limits Newton Abbot's cinema was proudly screening Laurence Olivier's *Henry V*. Lofty had not intended to waste any of his money on that in the first place.

9 • *France at Sea*

For the mass of Britishers, to succeed in leaving the European continent for any purpose at all in the first few years after war's end in 1945 constituted no mean achievement. Holiday travel abroad, when it applied, usually meant a brief trip to France, Holland or Belgium, though some enterprising spirits were known to have sampled the remoter pleasures of Scandinavia. Spain and Italy remained mysterious lands, virtually off limits until the mid-1950s. Popular tourism, with its voracious packaged multitudes, had not yet entered its stride. One day it would slay Bournemouth, Blackpool and Margate and their meagre attractions, but the time was not yet. Eastern Europe not only remained firmly shuttered against wanderers from the capitalist world, few Britishers evinced the inclination or need to spend their leisure so completely disconnected from the protection of HM Foreign Office.

Early in 1950 I wished to visit America. Politicians, business people, academics and those commanding the heights in the arts appeared to travel to the United States as casually as to the next borough. In my case every conceivable discouragement was placed in my way, for I belonged to the mass. Not that Britain was reluctant to let me go. America would not allow me in. Obtaining a visa entailed cross-examination by a US consular official, the exposure of one's psyche on to a complicated form and a humble demeanour, not to mention the waste of weeks.

It was a truth universally acknowledged that no run-of-the-mill European travelled to the United States with the intention of returning, least of all to a home country so desperately short of the good things of life as victorious Great Britain. America furthermore suspected applicants for a visa to be guilty of some act of moral turpitude and therefore liable to spread corruption to its native purity. You might well be a Communist, now or some time in the past, or keep company with one of those organisations pejoratively described as a 'front', with a less than enthusiastic opinion of the policies of the United States. Senator Joseph McCarthy of Wisconsin did not approve of such people.

The possibility inevitably troubled an American official's mind that you would possess no legitimate means of supporting your existence over there, thus taking bread from some poor American mouth. Finally, if you intended to settle in the United States, why were you concealing the fact? Uncle Sam maintained a careful watch against illegal immigrants stealing past the Statue of Liberty.

In those difficult times of post-war reconstruction under a draconian Labour government, an ordinary British citizen was not allowed to carry away more than five pounds in sterling, and no dollar currency. This gave the Americans additional reason for preferring us to stay away. A visitor was required to name a United States national as financial guarantor for the duration of his visit – another hurdle not always easily scaled.

Next, the problem of transportation. Nowadays, airlines practically beg you to board their planes. It was not then the case, civilian transatlantic flight being in its infancy. The few companies plying the New York route maintained priority lists in which the initials VIP were writ large, and I failed the qualification. None of the airlines wished to know me. It had to be a ship.

There again, the war had bequeathed a famine in tonnage, from which the great shipping lines had not yet recovered. A berth obtained in what survived was conferred as a favour, as was evidenced in the stolid faces one confronted across the enquiry counter. Your name would be recorded on a waiting-list that stretched vaguely into the middle distance. The magic word was contacts. I traced a contact, in a friend with a son employed by a shipping agency, and thus secured passage to

A Very British Subject

New York on the *De Grasse*, a single-class vessel of the French Line, for my little family complete with mother-in-law. Only on the day previous to embarkation did I obtain my American visa, secured after an urgent direct appeal to the United States ambassador by telegram. My Russian name had apparently given his menials pause. Our relatives on the other side would ensure that we would not end up in God's own country as vagabonds wandering the streets.

Until sailing for New York on the *De Grasse* I had presumed to understand France and the French. My pre-war English education had introduced me to the subject via textbook versions of the battles of Trafalgar and Waterloo and Napoleon's retreat from Moscow. Admittedly, the French excelled at cooking but, as I understood them, they were hopeless in choosing a constitution by which their country might be rationally administered. Across the Channel revolutions followed each other in bewildering fashion every couple of decades, while old hands at the governing game in Great Britain had thoroughly settled their own administrational problems by the Glorious Revolution, as long ago as 1688.

I should have known better, for I had spent a year in France before the war. But I had carried my prejudices with me and allowed no actual experience on the spot to tamper with them. That period had left me passionate about the wonders of Paris, its civilised café life and the exhilaration to be drawn from a glass of Bordeaux rouge. I had made good friends there, though only among the displaced tribal coteries, never with a native-born French citizen. Those I actually met came into my orbit in the course of purchasing a baguette or going about the business of registering as an alien. Such was the destiny of the foreigner in pre-war Paris, a city he only knew at its exciting centre. The residential suburbs remained an enigma, but he generally did not regard this as a deprivation.

The healing gift of time did not affect my negative impressions of France. No one, I had decided, could take seriously a nation fobbed off with such cambered country roads, or horse flesh masquerading as steak. Gospel forbade an Englishman from drinking French tap water. I recalled a street vendor in the rue de Rivoli extolling the virtues of some pathetic kitchen gadget, a new way of beating an egg, I believe. He terminated his eulogy of this great invention in clarion phrases: *ce n'est pas anglais, ce n'est pas americain, c'est français!* I felt sorry for them all, struggling to catch up with the age of technology. Britain as a whole, it is safe to say, shared my estimate of the French condition.

You could not but regard the people of this land with scorn, I told myself, as I dropped a couple of francs for a *pourboire* on the crochet table-cloth of my concierge for every little service, such as handing me a letter, or countersigning a *fiche* indicating change of address for filing at the prefecture. Oh, and those cold crowded trains stuck in sidings for hours during brief journeys of under 50 miles! Their public gardens were beautiful, but just try sitting on the grass!

In summation, I remembered France as a land creaking beneath its rusting bureaucratic machinery and masking gross incompetence with excessive, rather comical *politesse*. The nation's collapse in a matter of days after the German invasion of 1940, the chaos ensuing in the aftermath of war, the posture of pride and determination of a defeated people that actually intended to win their empire back, were among the subjects that served to increase my derision. Until the *De Grasse*.

It was February 1950 when I boarded the vessel, having discharged my final responsibility as a British citizen that same day: voting in the election that allowed Labour to scrape back to power with a majority of ten. Britain had not yet extricated itself from the mess of fighting a long war. In fact it edged perilously near to bankruptcy. Basic items of food continued to be rationed, the restoration of bombed cities had not even begun and the shortage of housing was keeping extended families together claustrophobically as though locked in a prison cell. Coal to warm freezing homes was dispensed meagrely against permits (we had had the return of the ice age in 1947), while the pubs ran out of beer, the tobacconists out of cigarettes, the workers out of will. The general human situation found vivid representation in that ubiquitous, sexless garment of neutral colour, the duffle coat.

My first surprise on board the *De Grasse* was the food, starting with breakfast; a banquet at every meal! It's not that I had forgotten such luxurious eating, I had never known it. This was quickly followed by a remark made by a deck steward to me. He was a man who plied the transatlantic route frequently, but a mere Frenchman still. He confessed how much he disliked New York, because, he said, it was so dirty. What, after Paris? That city had in the past bewitched me; but clean? Had he forgotten the mire clinging to the gutters on a rainy day around Les Halles? Had he never caught the aroma prevailing at the *pissoirs*, let alone the spectacle of men hurrying from those unsecluded conveniences fumbling with their dress, and the tramps sleeping rough, and the refuse piled high in the courtyards of the Third Arrondissement?

It amazed me that this steward could in one sweep condemn Broadway, Wall Street and Central Park, all of which I had studied from the comfort of a London cinema seat. Europe was crowded with people aching for the privilege of making a new life in America, and here was this underling of a second-rate nationality retailing offensive gossip against its greatest city. He could only be spurred by vulgar jealousy.

There was nothing austere or defeatist about the *De Grasse*. She floated over the waves so majestically she could have been re-enacting the pleasures of the Second Empire. It disturbed me to observe how many French passengers, even the men, changed into formal clothes for dinner, while the British (and Americans) assumed that what you wore for breakfast served the day through. How did they manage it? We British had only recently been released from the tyranny of clothing coupons, and deemed ourselves lucky to possess a second suit. This was no summer cruise indulged in by the idle rich, or comfortably off elderly! People were not yet crossing the Atlantic for their pleasure, but almost exclusively on purposes relating to such serious preoccupations as trade, a family reunion, a lecture tour, or that important one-way passage in life, emigration.

France at Sea

My corduroy trousers had been carrying me through countless social and professional engagements at home without giving offence. Here this dependable garment marked me out as an inferior being, possibly a stowaway in clumsy disguise. I rarely used my second pair of trousers during the voyage, intending to preserve them for a grand entry upon New York. However, I graced the gala evening preceding disembarkation by changing into these trousers and setting the effect off with a shirt of brightly coloured checks. These preparations earned me an angry reproof from the head steward, unique surely in the experience of any paying passenger in an ocean-going liner. 'You should be ashamed', he said, in his murderous version of English. 'Regard those gentlemen wearing their *smoking*, and you attend our farewell celebration in that attire.'

It had come to this. The French were now teaching the nation of Savile Row how to dress! Having anticipated a servility more appropriate to a people whom we had but recently liberated from enemy occupation, I was mortified by this aspect of the deterioration of the *Entente Cordiale*. Here was an example of the tables impudently overturned. We constituted the have-nots, the unfortunates, the nation without a change of clothing, and so feckless withal as to tolerate our government sanctioning pocket money of not more than five pounds for a sojourn in the New World.

More, those in command of our lives on this ship had determined that no one privileged to sail on the *De Grasse* would disembark without a lesson in the glories of their graceful language. English was a minority dialect on that vessel, the patois of an inferior race. No crew member deigned to employ it. The only English thing acceptable was our currency, of which we had woefully little, and that carefully husbanded so as to be able to distribute the minimal regulation tips commensurate with self-respect. Crew members only spoke English in the course of a financial transaction of profit to themselves.

That gala evening, so brilliantly accoutred it could have been July the Fourteenth at the Elysée Palace, gave an enduring lesson in the perils of underestimating the French. They marshalled all the male passengers of my unfortunate nationality, together with the few Americans, on to a central point. There, to the accompaniment of the orchestra, we were made to sing a popular ballad in French. Patiently, those of us ignorant of the tongue were taken through the verses of the song line by line, bar by bar. We ourselves were proud of our own language, as in the natural order of things, since the world was required to employ it or suffer the consequences. Now, I concluded, we were being rendered the victims of sheer chauvinism, a sentiment that in Britain had died with the air raids, and eggs reconstituted from powder, and window curtains created out of dyed parachute material, and Mr Clement Attlee as Prime Minister.

In retrospect, I thank the *De Grasse* for rectifying my insular English disease, complacency. Moreover, I remember the crew with affection for the cleverest pun ever to reach my ears. It was perpetrated by our dining-room waiter on the first evening that my mother-in-law Rebecca was well enough to join us for the meal. Hitherto the voyage had been turbulent, a land-lubber's ordeal. Sylvia's mother had been confined to her cabin during four days of acute distress as she awaited the calming of the seas. She had not been seen by our waiter.

Now, as we drew near to the American continent, the violent movement of the ship abated, the waves grew docile, and Rebecca made her début. The waiter looked, smiled, and ceremoniously bowed. Then, with one slight gesture towards the sea, and another to that grand old lady, he observed: 'Belle mer, belle-mère.' A happy ending to a most educational voyage, with forgiveness all round.

10 • Biting the Apple

What most powerfully impressed me on my first glimpse of New York City from the Atlantic approaches early in 1950 were the motor cars. I had expected there to be lots of them, but not in every variety of colour. Hitherto my experience had been of two kinds of vehicle, black civilian, brown military. It had not occurred to me that they could be painted otherwise. Now, as they streaked along the highway bordering the Hudson river these motor cars formed a horizontal, mechanical rainbow, a symbol of the divine joined to the profane in the Land of the Free.

Once disembarked, a nervous tension compelled me to remain stock-still long enough to take in the people. It was as though I was searching for another message. However, banality took over. Men had virtually banished headgear in England, but here I observed that they all wore hats. And no wonder. The winter wind blows icy cold in New York. Then my stare concentrated on a newspaper vendor; nothing extraordinary about him, except that he was smoking a cigar.

As we took up our positions in a long line on Pier 14 and docilely waited for some two hours at customs and passport control, not daring to protest lest this result in our prompt deportation, hawkers wandered up and down the queue. They had no refreshments to peddle, nor anything else tangible. Each of them held pencil and pad at the ready and encouraged us to do immediate business with Western Union by sending a wire back home announcing our safe arrival.

Whatever your actual purpose in coming to America, you were simultaneously verifying the mythology. In Europe we were still calling them Yanks, a breed loaded with ludicrously ostentatious affluence that intrigued without as yet changing the way the rest of us thought. They had given the old continent the Marshall Plan, which many Europeans disapproved of, suspecting a catch. Their paper currency equated with gold, and was described by the economists as hard. Years later the cinema would portray the carryings on of aliens invading from another planet. For the moment the Yanks fulfilled the phenomenon.

I therefore strove somewhat hastily in that first experience of New York to connect up all I had witnessed and confirm the stereotype: languid port officials, ambulatory telegram salesmen, newsboys with cigars, and reduce them to a generality in their coloured automobiles – people all of the same brand of canned flesh rolling off the production line. As this outsider perceived it, employment knew no hierarchies among the natives. Every additional dollar was worth the effort, so make it while you can and spend it before some bastard puts a tax on it. This appeared quite fair to be going on with, though needless to admit, each new day afterwards compelled a modification of my opinions.

We were deposited among relatives in a small, low building like a miniature warehouse. Squeezed between garages housing huge trucks, this building stood adjacent to the junction of West 18th Street with Tenth Avenue in Lower Manhattan. It served as home and office for an infant publishing enterprise. Much of the work was performed round the kitchen table, quite close to a gas cooker on one side and a bed on the other. And here our relatives laboured long hours, babies crying, kettle steaming, visitors from England sometimes sleeping, for that extra dollar. At intervals my American brother-in-law (this was our first encounter) lifted his head to share his grandiose American dreams with the family.

He told of those dreams with the assurance defining a man who carried his atmosphere with him, as if excluding all other possibilities from his calculations. I heard out his schemes of future achievement in silent deference, though reservations sprang to my head as I helped to address circulars and parcel up his cheap booklets for the post. Every morning he opened the post to collect the cash accompanying the few positive replies. The money totalled the household's running expenses for the day. My brother-in-law's career does not belong to this story. Suffice to say he had reached these shores in the late 1920s from Manchester, a fatherless teenager without education. Within a decade following our first meeting he would be regularly flying first class to Europe and putting up at the most de luxe hotels.

We had arrived on a Saturday evening and West 18th Street had entered its deserted weekend. The only sounds to be heard the next day emanated from across the street. I peeped from the window to discover the source: a saloon bar, bearing a prominent sign advising that the establishment admitted no unaccompanied women. And the noise? A recording continually booming a popular, brassy song, 'If I knew you were coming I'd have baked a cake'. The deafening refrain did not cease throughout the entire Sunday. Later that same day a man lay on the pavement outside, dead drunk or perhaps dead. It transpired to be death. A struggle? Some wound incurred previously? Natural causes? The body was efficiently removed and I did not enquire.

Family intimacy establishes rituals and invites communication in code. My eyes made contact with the eyes of my wife Sylvia, relaying a signal. Rude as it might appear, we needed to escape on to the streets of New York for a while and catch our breath.

'But you won't know where to go', my wife's sister warned. 'Will you find your way back?' She had overlooked the explorer tradition in the British, forgetting her own experience in our women's army as a signaller in obscure country hide-outs. In years gone by she had walked the streets of London in darkest blackout undeterred, in and out of air-raids, to return home unerringly and unscathed.

We took 18th Street in our stride, inhaling the sharp, cold air, and crossed the avenues, Ninth to Fifth. Along our route the prominence of rusting fire escapes, hanging precariously off the faces of tall buildings, were reminders of the hazards to life on a small island with people spilling over every inch of space. Safety overrode aesthetics. What were known at home as little corner shops described themselves here as food markets and meat markets, unfamiliar employment of a common noun. Men's outfitters advertised shirts at nineteen dollars for a dozen. Who in Britain purchased those garments except one at a time? The bargains astounded me.

Fifth Avenue of course implied style, fashionable department stores and upper crust window-shoppers. We turned here to investigate. This being the lower end, nothing evoked recognition. A modest-looking café appeared open for business. Hopefully, we decided to award it our patronage for light refreshment. An impeccably attired waiter beckoned us to a table, and before hearing our order he brought iced water and welcomed us with a speech that indicated his pronounced difficulty with the English language.

Since so little remained of the five pounds allowance granted to each of us by the British government, we prudently restricted ourselves to coffee, abstaining from a pastry. The coffee arrived efficiently, and very acceptable it proved. The thought occurred to me that this smiling waiter was according us more conversation than our custom warranted. I decided he was a friend, and asked, in all humility, whether it was the practice to leave a tip with so minute a transaction.

The gentle condescension in the waiter's tone was touching. 'Don't worry about it', he replied reassuringly. 'We all begin as strangers in New York. In time you will find your way around.' Our way of speaking English being just one more impaired European accent to his ears, he had taken it for granted that we too were immigrants, more recent than himself, and consequently still very green. My brother-in-law was tickled when we reported on our walk. 'So for a coffee you had to choose Longines', he said. 'Pretty fancy.' He never drank coffee, I discovered. His Mancunian preference for tea survived still.

While Hollywood held chief responsibility for giving us

Biting the Apple

America – the old Hollywood purveying an idealised America – realism was studiously eliminated from anything designed for mass entertainment, and particularly so in the early 1950s. With rare exceptions film stars buried their ethnic origins in impeccable Anglo-Saxon names. The only coloured people seen on the silver screen were placed there for humour, or to illustrate their dog-like devotion to their white masters. Dance orchestras and their soloists could be shiny black and, subjoined to their musical instruments, were generously allowed to perform in hotels and restaurants reserved for a white clientele. Hollywood thus provided the European with all he needed for instruction in the ways of this free young country. Almost unnoticed, down town on the west side of Manhattan the Puerto Ricans were opening their barber shops. The process by which they, and the blacks (then described as Negroes), would find a collective voice to articulate their own aspirations still lay in the future, awaiting a leader.

One of our friends from England had married a Harvard graduate employed in the city's social services. Formerly, at literary gatherings arranged in the upstairs rooms of Clerkenwell pubs and advertised on the back page of the *New Statesman*, Denise Levertov would self-consciously produce an occasional poem from her handbag to test out on like aspirants to the printed page. We took an early opportunity to visit Denise and her husband Mitchell Goodman in their home, termed a cold water walk-up, high in a Greenwich Village tenement.

Greenwich Village, its streets bearing names rather than ordinals, in fact slightly resembled Clerkenwell in this period of limbo between its raffish pre-war character and the extravagances of its hippie age. Families lived among the jazz clubs regularly opening and closing, and Washington Square Park, as sedate as its Kensington equivalent though not a tithe as attractive, safely harboured frolicking children of the neighbourhood. To be sure, the Village claimed the prerogatives of an artists' quarter, though New York still frowned on overt bohemianism and regarded blue jeans adopted for weekday attire as bizarre. The two rooms occupied by our friends and their baby gave little indication of a mad, mad world and a coming cultural explosion.

Considerable disorder distinguished the little apartment, there being no cupboards for clothes or other possessions. An interesting contraption suspended over the kitchen sink could drop a curtain. By stepping into the sink and pulling a string, relative privacy for a shower would result. Generally, crockery filled the sink. Posters, their corners peeling, decorated the walls, food was consumed wherever a place to sit became available, the child clamoured and old copies of a magazine called *Partisan Review* lay spread over the floor together with children's picture-books and last Sunday's edition of the *New York Times*. In this environment Denise Levertov, who was hoping shortly to acquire a baby's push-chair and thus, she informed us, 'emancipate myself', would steal a moment to write her poetry. Anyone in the know would understand from the magazine that this abode sheltered a couple of New York's educated radicals.

America did not lack for Communists at that time. Radicals of David Dubinsky's garment workers union openly indulged in those internecine conflicts that have always served as relaxation for the Left. Being impotent they were deemed not too objectionable. This couple, however, could have easily qualified for the attentions of Congressmen already suspecting witchcraft among more intellectually favoured middle classes.

His social welfare work took Mitchell into Harlem, and he invited us to join him for a day out there. My wife Sylvia and I would go separately, apparently social workers too. The arrangement suited us, for we had a baby of our own and one parent could care for him in the absence of the other. We had already inspected Times Square, decaying Coney Island, Brooklyn Bridge and Chinatown; now we would see Harlem from the inside. Here lived a goodly proportion of the population of a city that Walt Whitman had described as 'the directest proof yet of successful democracy'.

The subway brought us to 125th Street. Mitchell had no

clients among the billiard halls, food and furniture stores there, though the immense emporium of Edelstein's, the pawnbrokers, spoke volumes to any visitor with an interest in sociological research, as did the expensive beauty parlours where the 'kink' could be removed from tight black hair. We were bound for 127th Street, and picked our way between the children playing on the staircase of an old building. Mitchell rang a bell and we entered a ménage less deserving of the description than my own in the old London slum that had bred me. A man lay asleep on what presumably was the only large bed. A young woman held one child in her arms, while another lay in its cot.

Mitchell was answered with a blank stare by the woman as he questioned her regarding the family's situation and needs. At length she spoke. Yes, she'd been able to pay the rent. The man asleep? Not her husband, she had none. This man worked at night and he paid her to sleep here during the day. 'It's known as hot bed, a common practice', Mitchell enlightened me in a whisper. But there were no bed-clothes in the cot; the child lay on a bare mattress.

'We got plenty of bedding', said the woman, 'in the laundry downstairs.'

'Have you any toys for the children? I can get you some.'

'They don't need none. They're alright. Happy kids.'

We departed for the next address on his list, another room in another tenement, with a gaping hole beneath a window. 'It's okay here', the mother assured Mitchell. 'Except for the rats. The landlord done nothing about it.'

The procedure continued, and almost everywhere we were greeted by the same strong negatives. 'I can supply all kinds of their needs out of the city budget', Mitchell told me, 'but few of them will accept anything but their basic welfare money. My report will include an assessment of their living conditions, and order a visit by the Department of Health. Nothing significant will happen. They won't have the authorities poking around.'

Back on 125th Street, a cortège of Cadillacs signified the

funeral of a local black millionaire. The automobiles were privately owned, not hired. Harlem's most flourishing industry was the numbers racket, a shady lottery engaging the entire population. The community's rich lived among the show-business celebrities on Sugar Hill, above 140th Street.

White people intent on recreation still made for Harlem in the early 1950s, for the music, the night clubs featuring noted Negro performers, and for specialised sexual thrills. Drug peddling had begun to operate openly on 131st Street, though marijuana had yet to achieve its later acceptability among middle-class whites.

Observing that in this portion of New York City mounted police were strongly in evidence, I questioned Mitchell regarding the docility of the poor. 'Aren't you afraid these people will one day turn on you?' He did not think it likely. 'When there's trouble the police arrive in strength and hit out. They do it to the white folks too, of course, but not so hard. When it happens in a white neighbourhood it gets into the papers. Black people expect that kind of treatment, it doesn't make news. Once in a while, though, they conduct a "shoving day". On a signal, the men come downtown and shove the white passers-by, as if by accident. But it's co-ordinated.'

I was experiencing the 'Big Apple' (the band leader Cab Calloway's appellation for Harlem and already applied to the city as a whole) when the phrase denoted that here anything desirable was possible: not too much gang warfare, little violence on the subway, the streets safe to walk at night, the term 'mugging' still waiting to be coined. I succumbed to the spell of its incredible variety. Given that the race question was germinating into an issue without sign of resolution, New York offered friendship to the stranger, classlessness that neutralised social snobbery, and a delicious, perfectly served meal for the price of an English plate of fish and chips. Its public library on 42nd Street was a bookworm's wonderland, surely the best in the world. The street corner magazine stalls proved an embarrassment of intellectual riches.

In 1950 you paid a nickel for the ferry to Staten Island, and not much more to stand atop the Empire State building above the clouds. There was little greenery in Manhattan compared to London, and no public toilets. But cinema houses had begun segregating the smokers, and one could, without difficulty, sit close to Eleanor Roosevelt while she chaired a committee of the United Nations in its old building at Flushing Meadow. Then there was the American vocabulary: dozens of expressions unknown as yet in Britain, but when they subsequently turned up in the *Evening Standard* I greeted them as old friends. The term 'workshop' amused me, because of its application here to what we called discussion groups.

Accompanied by Sylvia I returned on one occasion to Harlem for an 'autograph party' – another of those expressions new to me. Above a bookshop on 125th Street Langston Hughes was launching his *Simple Speaks His Mind*. With all the drinks and conversation, we hardly realised we were the only white people present. Langston Hughes had invented this rough character Simple, whose street-wise philosophy would in time be distilled into a manifesto of black liberation. In the meantime the term Negro provoked no offence and, as we introduced ourselves, one of the Harlem sophisticates wondered, 'Surely London can't be so provincial as New York!'

Langston Hughes signed our copy of his book and it was past midnight when we took the subway back to our family on 18th Street. We went to many white parties during our stay in New York but nowhere did we feel less like outsiders than at this gathering of the Harlem literati. Some years would elapse before I could visit New York again. By this time the blacks had already begun working on their identity, via Afro hairstyles and the vaunted beauty of their race. I took care to leave Harlem before darkness fell.

On a third visit in 1968, I omitted use of the subway and a journey to Harlem altogether. Most of my relatives and friends had retreated from Manhattan. I date that first acquaintance with New York in 1950 as terminating an era. Gentle Langston Hughes gave way to James Baldwin and the fire he prophesied. Denise Levertov, divorced from Mitchell, truly emancipated herself to become a leading American poet and woman liberationist.

The British masses no longer regarded New York as a remote, exotic shore. Many could easily afford a holiday there with a courtesy self-drive car thrown in. But the Bronx had become a second Harlem which you drove through at your peril. America continues to police the world, though it still fails to protect its own citizens venturing on the subway.

11 • God's Footstool

The man is too great, I was informed, for any writer to do justice to his achievements in a single volume of biography. Another admirer, with skull cap and patriarchal beard, reinforced the view: 'He is an instrument of the Messiah, and we cannot gauge the full extent of his personality.' I recalled an heiress in a family owning the largest chain of department stores in England who confessed her sole ambition as being allowed into his home to cook his meals.

Since this was Jerusalem, and the year 1953, I could not suppress the thought that its inhabitants lived a degree or two nearer to God than the rest of us. I had been commissioned to write the life of their Prime Minister, David Ben-Gurion, and perceived that I must begin by adjusting to a different reality. Jerusalem, according to the Jewish mystics, was the footstool of the Lord. Ben-Gurion had successfully defended its newer section against an alliance of six invaders. Could I make a book of such a man? Could I complete any book? This first biography of Ben-Gurion in any language would also be my first.

The Eden Hotel (second best in the Holy City after the King David) faced scruffy Hillel Street close by Zion Square, near to the intersection of King George V Avenue and the Jaffa Road. It was late evening when I booked in, and the hotel stood eerily silent. The night clerk barely proffered me a glance. I had few acquaintances in the city, none of them intimates, and no known relatives. I could not speak the language except after a limited fashion. Alienation set in, like something eaten cold but not digested in the pit of my stomach. A crackle of rifle shots reached my ears from the unseen ramparts surrounding the Old City.

Jerusalem was not simply divided in the physical sense. A fence of tangled wire marked a narrow no man's land littered with rubbish. It separated two armies, two civilisations, two peoples living in different epochs. There was fear and there was hatred, while each faithfully believed God was its special, omnipotent ally. On one side of the barrier the people cherished a tradition going back to a desert prophet of the seventh century. The others could summon a hinterland of sentiment spanning millennia and reaching geographically across the Atlantic, where it was manifested by regular fund-raising banquets at the Waldorf-Astoria Hotel in New York. So much space, though in this room at the Eden I experienced a surreptitious claustrophobia, and needed the sight of a street.

Quite a modern hotel, the Eden boasted a lift. Eyeing it, I descended by the stairs. Mechanical things, I had been advised, did not always operate efficiently even in the most progressive cities of the Orient. Lifts sometimes stick between floors. Surely I was the solitary guest in this establishment, and could be entombed. Human sounds, so welcome to a lonely stranger, carried from the direction of Zion Square. There, a young, jostling crowd testified to boisterous life. They seemed in the main Oriental Jews, their origin plainly detectable. They laughed as they talked and licked ice-cream. A group hung around a board game I had last seen in my East London childhood – Crown and Anchor. With *their* money? I had understood the currency to be so inflated as to render it virtually worthless. No, the coins were accepted. Light shone from a corner café, its beam a welcome.

Entering the café, it pleased me to find most of the tables occupied, and as I took a seat a young man, quite mature though probably a student, spoke at once, in American English. Such is the way in his country, easily and without inhibition. His tone suggested sorrow, as though he suffered. 'I would never have believed it', he said.

'What do you mean?'

'I would never have believed it. Out in the square I was

God's Footstool

accosted by this girl. She wanted me to go with her. A prostitute here in Jerusalem!'

'And you're shocked?'

'No, not that. I'm from Philadelphia. But to think that here, in the Jewish State, the first in almost two thousand years, they have whores! In Philadelphia it's hard to find a Jewish prostitute. Yet in the Holy City . . .' His voice trailed away, signifying incredulity and distress. 'I'm thinking of taking her back with me', he stated earnestly, 'and giving her a fresh start. Zionism, Zion Square after a miracle, heroic defenders in war, you come to Israel and meet a young *prostitute*!'

I recognised that emotion of betrayal. The Zionist apparatus was geared to the proposition that in Israel the Jews formed a superior breed. Liberated from the shadow of anti-semitism, dedicated to their soil, they drained marshland and made the desert bloom. Many of them established villages conducted according to the principles of the purest socialism and were reconciled to defending their new way of life to the last man and woman. All this under their charismatic guide, David Ben-Gurion, himself a pioneer but additionally an oracle and brilliant military commander. Well, nothing spoken about Israel was the whole truth, and nothing a total lie. But visiting Jews, in the dramatic period of state building just a few years following the War of Independence in 1948, closed their eyes to everything here except what they desired to see, and it had the colour of roses. Leaving the perplexed American to make his own discoveries, I returned to the hotel, read my notes, checked over my contacts and sank into uneasy sleep. Tomorrow I would be looking for myself.

Doubtless Jerusalem was ideally located for a capital city in the days of the biblical David. In this partitioned Palestine it tilted precariously from a promontary cornered in a compressed salient of the Judaean hills. The kingdom of Jordan lay immediately to the north, south and east, from which a descent of 15 miles led to the metallic surface of the Dead Sea, lowest point on the globe. The Israelis had access to the southern half of the lake via a detour by way of Beersheba. The Jaffa Road exit from Jerusalem took you direct to the hot-house sprawl of Tel-Aviv and the coast. However, should your vehicle wander off the track to get stuck in a valley you might find yourself in enemy territory.

Amazingly, the hazards appeared not to trouble the Jerusalemites, except that they tended to retire to bed early, since little in the form of night life existed. During the day cabinet ministers walked the streets unprotected. Ramblers with their picnic baskets wandered into the hills in search of Roman coins. And, Zion Square excepted, there pervaded a general atmosphere of tranquillity, polite conversation and reverence. You could not visit a cinema on the Sabbath nor catch a bus, for traffic lights and all municipal services ceased. On the seventh day you might hail a taxi or drive your own car, provided the vehicle stayed clear of Mea Shearim, the neighbourhood occupied by strictly fundamentalist Jews who refused to recognise secular authority in any shape. The pace was unhurried, and a stroll down King George Avenue in the crisp evening light resembled the *passeggiata* of a serene Italian township.

Such was New Jerusalem on the outside. Beneath the surface lay a nervy, brittle Jewish citizenry, clearly divided between Orientals and Westerners. You told the difference by who performed the unskilled jobs – invariably Orientals. The Westerners divided again into a Russian power structure and a Mittel-European civil service; then further according to degrees of religious formalism: strictly orthodox, lesser orthodox and agnostic. In 1953 all of Israel embraced a population of just above a million, hardly greater than Birmingham. Ben-Gurion was a Russo-Polish immigrant, somewhat agnostic and at the summit of the power structure, almost a benevolent despot. Most of the people worshipped him. But not those of the extreme Right and far Left, nor the members of his own Labour Party whom he had discarded on his way to the top. They detested him.

I had sent letters to the Prime Minister before my arrival, none of which had been answered. After a couple of days in

Jerusalem, gazing at its sights, familiarising myself with its topography, acting the polite Englishman abroad by trying to stand patiently in line at the *bureau de change*, I discovered how things got done in this country. It was not by correspondence.

Letters were unnecessary, because whatever was deemed important in the administration of Israel was strung along King George Avenue. Government offices in those early days of statehood could be above a travel agency, or within a modest hotel, or behind the windows of a private house. In the side streets buildings with a Turkish façade sheltered individual ministries. At least one of them had seen a previous existence as a Christian mission. Enquiry desks were rare. You walked in and stated your business to the first person encountered.

King George (no one bothered with 'Avenue') gained its designation of course in the days when British Mandatory officials were apt to confuse Palestine with the out-stations of their colonial empire. The Jews liked the name and Arab objections, such as they were, went unheeded. The Arabs had still not properly awakened from a passivity bred by centuries of alien rule. Tree-lined King George meandered uncertainly before it crossed Ben-Yehuda Street. My hotel lay between the two and I regularly caught myself out in one of them thinking it was the other.

I should have known better, for King George exuded character whereas Ben-Yehuda earned the money, from its banks, dress shops, picture galleries and falafel stands. Moreover, King George had a yawning gap between the buildings like a huge London bomb site, destined for transformation one day into a park. Formerly a Muslim burial ground, it offered a vista upon foreign territory beyond the barrier, over the city walls and, faintly, the Mount of Olives. Every passer-by slowed down to look.

More empty plots of land, their ownership concealed in ancient records of Ottoman property law, separated other buildings the length of the avenue. A stately corner edifice, surmounted by the Virgin, crowned King George at its southern end. This was Terra Sancta, belonging to the Franciscans and leased to the Hebrew University, whose campus, though inviolate on Mount Scopus, lay through Jordanian territory and was therefore inaccessible to the Jews. According to Josephus, the legions of Titus had encamped on Mount Scopus during the Roman seige of Jerusalem. British soldiers now sleep for ever on this spot, in their military cemetery.

My researches would take me up and down King George a hundred times, and frequently into an imposing pile, overpowering in size, called the Jewish Agency building. It testified to the role played by the international instruments of Zionism. Designed horseshoe style, the edifice took a spacious forecourt within its grasp. Persons of great importance parked their cars there.

It speaks volumes that the Prime Minister and his staff were compressed into a small corner of this Kremlin. Additionally, Ben-Gurion had established various scientific and cultural sub-departments under his aegis, all requiring accommodation for an assistant or two in this confined space. Entered by a side door in a street adjacent to King George, the Prime Minister's headquarters was guarded by a young soldier who evinced the barest interest in one's business. I walked in, not doubting for a moment that English would be understood there equally with Hebrew.

As it happened, English rendered communication in Israel more effective than Hebrew. A native speaker could be greeted with discourtesy as 'one of us' – another Jew with a grouse or a bee in his bonnet. As likely as not he would be passed around from one busy official to another, days dragging into weeks. English, on the other hand, gave a cachet and roused a more willing ear. Artists, journalists and academics, Jew or gentile and coming from wherever, preferred the language. All Israelis worked at making a good impression on the foreigner with status. They had enemies enough and had no wish to increase the number. However, diplomatic envoys were rarely to be seen in Jerusalem, except unofficially, for the city had still to receive recognition as the national capital. The embassies remained with their languages in Tel-Aviv.

Even to the least devout among the Jewish people, the Hebrew language carried essences from its spiritual origins. The early rabbis taught that Adam spoke to Eve in the sacred tongue, and God to Moses. Ben-Yehuda Street received its name from the idealist who turned Hebrew into an everyday vernacular, late in the nineteenth century. Ben-Yehuda's son was its first natural speaker in modern times (as a consequence, in maturity he preferred French). Some Jews to this day believe that to speak Hebrew would profane it. The language also served as a quasi-secret cryptograph to those who knew it really well, and particularly so by native-born Israelis of the younger generation. Those concerned with military policy and intelligence would obviate leakages by using no other. In fact, few Jews of the Diaspora thoroughly understood the ancient tongue in its modern revival. But some Arabs made the mastery of Hebrew an effective entry into the Israeli mentality.

Youth, they say, speaks readily to youth, and I was still young enough to be put immediately at ease on entering the Prime Minister's headquarters by the man seated in an outer office. Evidently he had time and patience in abundance for me. Yes, he knew the name, remembered my letters and understood the purpose of my presence in the country. He might have passed as a civil servant of no great seniority, yet transpired to be the key to access to the Prime Minister. Yitzhak Navon occupied the position of personal secretary and aide to the leader. However, he was not hopeful. Ben-Gurion had apparently been approached by several British and American publishers for his story, and hitherto had refused them all.

Navon belonged to a prominent family of Sephardic origin tracing a line back to the expulsion from Spain in 1492. A land-owning grandfather initiated the construction of the Jerusalem–Jaffa railway, the first in Palestine, so if the Jews acknowledged an aristocracy, Navon would be inscribed there. He bridged the two Jewish cultures, eastern and western, and would one day rank high in a far greater population and a much expanded area, with all Jerusalem conquered. He ultimately achieved election as State President, and at this writing the only incumbent of that office at home in Arabic.

For the present, Navon confessed to considerable scepticism regarding my project. He was dubious of my success in securing his chief's co-operation where so many others had failed. He shared the near-universal attitude of veneration towards Ben-Gurion, though with more reason than most, since nearness can reveal facets of a character that tarnish the image. The questions Navon put to me obviously served to test me out: credentials, competence, sympathy with Zionism. Fortunately, the publisher commissioning the biography was well known to the authorities, for George Weidenfeld of London had earlier been enlisted for a year as adviser to Israel's first president, Chaim Weizmann.

The amicableness of the interview, and indeed the general informality of this modest equivalent of 10 Downing Street, soothed all apprehensions. Had I any such intention, I could easily have planted a bomb. Navon agreed to refresh his chief's memory regarding the proposed biography, though he warned of delay. In the meantime I should await a call. All this left me with a suspicion that I might wait as had other authors before me, for ever. Navon promised to contact me with a yea or nay. But I descended into King George sunshine uncertain of my ground and uneasy with the impression I had made as a foreign writer. How dare I aim to usurp precious time from a man engaged in transforming this notch of the Middle East, its existence disputed, its borders undefined, its prospective immigrants still to be persuaded, into a modern state?

Naturally, I was determined meanwhile to talk with anybody who had the slightest acquaintance with Ben-Gurion. He had lived in Palestine since 1906, when it constituted an insignificant satrapy ruled from Constantinople, and had attained leadership through a classic road: labourer turned trade union official, street agitator, conference orator, party leader, guerilla strategist and propagandist in the capitals of the world. His roots therefore stretched back to the élite generation that really had drained marshland in the Jezreel valley and established those farming communes, the *kibbutzim*, that endowed the national endeavour with its ingredient of self-sacrifice. Comrades from those times, if less exalted in station, could be discovered here, in Jerusalem; more, in the towering structure next door.

The Jewish Agency in all its many tentacles might well have been the largest employer in the country. It purchased and reafforested land, housed and integrated immigrants, administered archives, conducted tourism, negotiated foreign loans and despatched emissaries to communities overseas. It owned a bank and published books. Its magnitude alone encouraged criticism, and people spoke of the Agency as a second, unelected government. Ben-Gurion had been its chairman during the British Mandate, when it challenged Whitehall to open the gates wide while Whitehall took the strain of swelling Arab animosity. Here I stood at the Agency's headquarters, where, I had been informed, a comrade from the Prime Minister's pioneering days worked in some humble capacity.

Joshua Schlingbaum sat in a tiny office at the end of a corridor on the third floor. A shrunken figure, he appeared to register surprise at the appearance of a visitor, like a creature secure in its jungle abode until startled by the sound of gunshot. Papers lay spread over every surface, presumably aids to his function as editor of an information bulletin in Yiddish. That language was still to be heard in a few isolated corners of the Diaspora. Schlingbaum's English being minimal, I explained myself as best I could. Solemnly he replied.

'This is a great labour indeed, that you are engaged upon. A most significant labour. So much research.' His Yiddish, uttered in staccato accents, bore the archaic flavour of a bygone literary age. 'And I would be glad to help you. To my regret, I cannot claim that I know Ben-Gurion well.' He fell silent, evidently listing the occasions of their meeting in his mind. After deliberation, he went on: 'True, I did know him in the old days, but not, as you might say, to talk to.'

As I prepared a polite departure he gave a little jump. 'Wait! Herzkovitz! He's the man for you. A friend of the Prime Minister. They worked together. Tell him Joshua sent you.'

I was grateful. 'Thank you. Where can I find Mr Herzkovitz?'

'At the Café Rehavia. He plays chess there every afternoon. A fine player. Just mention my name.'

Little difficulty beset my search for the Café Rehavia. Everyone seemed to patronise it. To reach the Rehavia district I proceeded down King George, turned sharp right at Terra Sancta and almost immediately came upon a discreetly prosperous enclave of leafy streets and solid villas of Bau-art dignity. Cypresses cast deep shadows upon pocket-size front gardens. Together with its air of middle-class assurance, Rehavia proclaimed the fulfilment of the Zionist dream at its proudest. The district came into existence as the earliest modern residential quarter of the Jews outside Suleiman the Magnificent's sixteenth-century walls. The emperor Haile Selassie of Ethiopia made temporary sojourn here on his expulsion from the Coptic kingdom by Mussolini in 1935. Wealthy Arabs built in Rehavia too, though after 1948 their houses, embracing airy rooms with tall arched ceilings, had been divided into flats by the Custodian of Enemy Property and leased to such Jews as could afford them. Many street names in Rehavia testified to the fruits of Zionism's association with the British before the alliance went sour – Balfour Road, Plumer Square, Wingate Square, Laurence Oliphant Street (he was the eccentric who covered the Crimean War for *The Times* and subsequently devoted his life to preaching the Jewish restoration to the Holy Land).

Prior to the building boom of the 1930s, when Rehavia rose, the inhabitants of Jerusalem were more thoroughly intermingled, the slums of the poor springing up, or decaying down, cheek by jowl beside the gracious residences of the rich. Half a mile up the Gaza Road from Terra Sancta would lead to rocky, thinly cultivated terrain and a spectacular prospect for the eye. There, isolated in its saucer-shaped valley, the Byzantine Monastery of the Cross stood in fortress-like defiance. The monastery's walls shielded the place, tradition held, where grew the tree from which Christ's Cross was hewn.

Gaza Road was much altered now, a thoroughfare out of which more recent streets branched, some of them still unpaved. They bore names glorifying Russian worthies familiar to every student of Zionism though to no one else – Arlosoroff, Ussishkin, Jabotinsky, and the sages of yore, Abrabanel, Ibn Gabirol, Maimonides. The café I sought arranged its tables artfully to enjoy both sun and shade, for all the world a relaxed outpost of old Vienna. There I found Mr Herzkovitz, one of several elderly customers engrossed in the game of chess.

Decidedly a gentleman of the old Central European school, he beckoned me to a seat, unperturbed by the interruption. The mention of Ben-Gurion cast no magic spell over him. 'Whatever gave you the idea that I might be of assistance?' he asked, in impeccable English, though spoken deliberately as though read from a text. 'I know nothing of the man, except that my work comes within the scope of the Prime Minister's department.' The way he slurred over his employer's title it could have been any prime minister, William Pitt the Younger perhaps, or Bismarck.

Herzkovitz then fastened me with a promise whose unfulfilment leaves me slightly guilty to this day. 'I am charged with commissioning translations of the universal classical literatures into modern Hebrew.' He was barely taking his attention away from the chess-board. 'The problem is, many of the works are not available here, either in their original languages or in English translation. But you can help. You have them all in London.'

I visualised a gesture of no great effort in despatching a Chaucer perhaps, together with an anthology of Elizabethan poets, even a Swinburne thrown in for good measure. This was not what Herzkovitz had in mind. 'I need Aeschylus, Tacitus, Sophocles, Baudelaire, Dante, Flaubert, Racine, the *Mahabharata*, the Golden Bough, Lamartine . . .' He reeled them off, a librarian's catalogue. I had ceased to listen. I didn't know how many years Herzkovitz had left for his translation work punctuated with afternoon chess. I would be spending the rest of my life in the Charing Cross Road. Israeli schemes were always large in conception.

Returning to the Eden Hotel, any slight commitment to Herzkovitz fell from my mind. The place was abuzz. In the crowded lounge people were booking rooms, ordering dinner, and standing in close conversational groups. It was late Monday afternoon. Of course! We were already well into the working week, which in Israel began on Sunday. They were, most of them, members of Israel's parliament, the Knesset, come to Jerusalem for its regular sessions on Monday, Tuesday and Wednesday. The Knesset had as yet no building designed for its purpose. The establishment of the state saw a provisional council assembled in the Tel-Aviv museum, a small building that had once been the large home of its leading citizen. Ben-Gurion later declared Jerusalem the capital (scorning the displeasure of the United Nations) but where to accommodate the 120 Knesset members, its officials and security guards, a restaurant, in what to all intents then ranked as a backwater country town?

Along King George a bank headquarters was nearing completion, surmounted with a block of flats. This building was commandeered. So Israel's parliament meekly faced the street at pavement level, and except when the Knesset held its sessions one walked by without a second glance. Why Ben-Gurion, who was already laying blueprints for a new port to rival Haifa, and factories the length and breadth of the country, and commanding Stalin to open the Soviet prison gates, did not take over a chunk of the huge Jewish Agency building for his parliament struck me as rather odd.

Evidently the Eden served as the Knesset's dormitory on those three days every week. Parliamentarians attract lobbyists, journalists, handsome women and every brand of hanger-on. So it was at my hotel, which incidentally proved a perfect hunting ground for seekers after wisdom like myself. In fact, many Knesset members assessed me with equal curiosity, and I discovered that the name Ben-Gurion, dropped ever so casually, worked like an incantation that conjured excited attention hereabouts. I could have filled up my appointments diary there and then, for I was showered with invitations for dinner and to inspect *kibbutzim*, orphanages, irrigation pipes and the foundation of a concert hall. A man was introduced as the brain behind the bombing of the King David Hotel in 1946, and I spoke with a Brazilian Jewess reputed to have slept with half a dozen cabinet ministers. ('Not true!' exploded a young parliamentarian. Was he one of those she had turned down?)

My purposes required a picture of them as a collective, in their constitutional habitat: the debating chamber. This country was an infant unique in that early formative period for Middle Eastern states, before the Arabs had developed their economic muscle as lords of nigh-inexhaustible oil wealth. Though Israel was already an aching thorn in their Mediterranean side, neighbouring nations could barely raise a tremor of their apprehension on the world arena. Israel alone could be described as a democracy, hell-bent on modernisation. It sold no oil, but philanthropy, added to foreign loans and American subsidies, was generously funding new housing and industry, not to mention its military capability. Most of the Middle East remained sparsely inhabited desert, beneath which the oil kept western home fires burning with as yet little profit to the native occupants. Israel pressed on as if its neighbours would for all eternity lack a political vocabulary and brandish weapons left over from the First World War. The western powers, incidentally, were making the same miscalculation.

Subjects of debate in the Knesset ranged the world. Without much ado I therefore crossed King George where traffic had been provisionally diverted, to afford pedestrian access to the parliamentary worthies, and entered the building with the assurance of an elected member. Next step must be a pass to the Press gallery. The officer responsible for their issue, a Londoner known to me, sat in a cubby-hole virtually filled by his ample person, and he was doing several jobs at once.

The sight of Moshe Rosetti alone demonstrated for me the attraction for a British immigrant to living in Jerusalem. One became a somebody. Had Rosetti settled in Tel-Aviv or Haifa he would have melted into the population as another businessman, or another teacher, engineer, architect, etc. Here he was a key official in the administrative system. The Knesset functioned around him.

Rosetti's bureaucratic career had begun as a humble employee in the offices of the Stepney Borough Council, from which he had graduated as a lobbyist for the Zionist cause specifically directed to ensuring the support of the British Labour Party. He developed an expertise in parliamentary procedure as laid down by Erskine May. In Jerusalem he described himself as Clerk of the Knesset. Rosetti was in at the birth of this parliament. I knew I would encounter little difficulty in obtaining my Press pass.

The crowd gathered around Rosetti's small desk swamped him. Could all these men and women be journalists? Well, not quite, for some had other requests – for employment, for an interview with a member, or to obtain a seat for a distinguished visitor. Mostly they represented newspapers. The Press featured as one of Israel's flourishing growth industries, corresponding to the colourful proliferation of political parties. Rosetti kept his head above the clamour.

According to his book, no parliamentary system could equal the British. Rosetti hoped that in time an upper chamber would exist here too, perhaps open to membership by Jewish dignitaries of the Diaspora, with a liberal sprinkling of Nobel prizewinners, of which his people suffered no famine. But the Israeli population was still so small you might indeed compare the Knesset to the Stepney Borough Council, and if Rosetti dropped his guard he was known to admit that the talent approximated to the same. In the meantime he made the rules himself as he went along.

Within a decade the Knesset would be housed in its own specially designed building, classically colonnaded like the Parthenon, off the Gaza Road. Located in its landscaped grounds, murals would decorate the actual chamber, guards in abundance would attend, with identity checks for visitors a *sine qua non*. Its two large restaurants would sub-divide for meat and dairy dishes. This forum would never equal the spirit of the intimate assembly on King George, nor the excitement of making history – the first Sanhedrin in the Holy City since its destruction by the Romans. The old Sanhedrin legislated for the entire Jewish world; Knesset members occasionally spoke in the mistaken assumption that they performed likewise.

As I saw it, everything in the makeshift Knesset was up against a deficiency of space, all except the debating chamber itself, which appeared as deserted as habitually was the House of Commons in Westminster. Perhaps I might find the bar. There was no bar. The restaurant, however, was packed and obviously understaffed, most of its customers hailing the stressed waitresses for a glass of tea. The Knesset as a place of refreshment suffered from competition by the nearby Eden Hotel.

The Press gallery was reached by a short staircase that doubled as a noisy antechamber for those reporters unable to find a seat in their actual preserve. I secured a corner for standing room. In the chamber a Communist delegate, speaking almost to himself, pleaded with honourable members to defy American capitalism and make common cause with all the Arabs in helping them shake off the yoke of economic imperialism. That is, as far as I could follow his argument, for the full translation of his speech (obligingly provided by the Communist's secretary) revealed greater subtlety of argument and a genuine feeling that Israel was ignoring Arab aspirations at its peril. In the gallery none of the reporters seemed to listen, nor did I observe any of them using a notebook.

Israel was still in the period, and was for long afterwards, when Labour repeatedly triumphed as the largest party, though never by an absolute majority. The Left suffered, as everywhere, from fragmentation. The Speaker of the Knesset (but for Rosetti he would have been termed 'chairman') carried Labour's card. He nevertheless acknowledged a political tradition deviating from Ben-Gurion's, the difference undefinable in ideological terms yet clear-cut to their pioneering generation and its memories. However, to know Ben-Gurion one had to know Josef Sprinzak, ensconced here as guardian of parliamentary decorum.

Next morning at breakfast at the Eden I observed the Speaker seated alone. I had once met him in London engaged on a fund-raising tour among the Jewish community. This being Jerusalem, and impertinence being measured here otherwise than in the societies of the West, I approached him uninvited, and took a seat at his table. Sprinzak's account of the association between the two old comrades, and why they drifted apart, would increase my understanding of Ben-Gurion considerably.

When I reminded Sprinzak of our earlier brief encounter in London the conversation took a most unsatisfactory turn. He appeared to nurture some grudge against England, and particularly against its Jewish population. He was a short man with a walrus moustache that suggested a quick temper. 'You are very provincial over there', he declared in his picturesque version of the English language.

Somewhat taken aback, I enquired the reason for his verdict. 'You don't know how to treat people. When I come to New York a Press conference is immediately arranged. I am introduced to the members of Congress, and invited to lunch by the Vice-President at least. The *New York Times* writes an article. In England, nothing.' He snorted in recollection of successive affronts.

If this was the case, Sprinzak certainly had a point. The presiding officer of a foreign parliament merited attention from the Press on his visit; and surely someone might have alerted the Speaker of the House of Commons to spare a welcome to his opposite number from distant parts. He was doubtless performing some such courtesy daily.

I found it difficult to defend my community, my city, my country and their reception of the distinguished stranger. In an effort to stand my ground, I tried to explain to this man, of little obvious patience and suffering a wound to his *amour propre*, that London and New York were not the same. Did Sprinzak not realise that *The Times* of London functioned differently from its transatlantic namesake? The Jews of Britain were not simply a reduced version of their brethren in America. New York City had, in those days, about three times the number of Jews than all Israel, and the *New York Times* catered zealously to their interests. Over there the Jews could practically command the Vice-President, as did all other groupings aware of their electoral clout, while in London the Jews constituted a more discreet, if by no means silent, minority. I had no heart now to introduce the subject of Ben-Gurion, fearing to stir up a further diatribe.

Another Knesset member put me right about Sprinzak. 'No one mentions Ben-Gurion to him,' he told me. 'You daren't. He could have a heart attack. You were wise to keep off the subject.' I soon learned why. The rift between them first appeared with their respective attitudes to the Arabs in the early days. Ben-Gurion was even then convinced that a struggle for this soil would ensue, while Sprinzak favoured compromise. He wished to win Arab friendship by appreciation of their native susceptibilities.

The memory of that conflict still lingered as Ben-Gurion became all powerful and Sprinzak found himself side-tracked to the Speaker's chair. It revived passionately with the death of Chaim Weizmann, State President, in 1952. That too was merely an honorific office, and virtually belonged of right to the incumbent Speaker should it fall vacant. Ben-Gurion blocked Sprinzak's anticipated succession. He indicated that the man was not of the cast to bring esteem to the presidency. Who, then? No Israeli candidate would satisfy the Prime

Minister. His thoughts turned to Princeton University and the man universally revered as scientist and humanist – Einstein, the most distinguished refugee rendered stateless by Adolf Hitler. How appropriate to crown his life by reunion with his people in Jerusalem! Einstein turned the privilege down, whereupon Ben-Gurion's choice went to another old pioneering comrade, a man outside politics, Yitzhak Ben-Zvi. Sprinzak's friends never forgave Ben-Gurion. Plenty here to research for my biography, should it ever proceed. I had not as yet heard from Yitzhak Navon.

New Jerusalem hardly gave the impression in 1953 of being particularly modern. It had asserted itself rather haphazardly when it began on a rockstrewn patch of land outside the walled town. A windmill and terrace of cottages, built by the British philanthropist Moses Montefiore, inaugurated his dream a hundred years before to establish the original Jewish population in agriculture. However, the smallholding experiment proved short-lived, for Jerusalem suffers a chronic water shortage. In its place a mosaic of neighbourhoods arose in which tight little groups found sleepy residence, taking in each other's laundry, baking each other's bread, teaching each other's children the holy life and collectively surviving by subventions begged from abroad. Christian and Muslim sects put down roots too, and the three co-existed according to the rules of a previous age, defying change.

While awaiting a signal from Yitzhak Navon I acquainted myself with every feature of this so-called New City. It stimulated my sensations as none other I had seen, a surprise round every corner. Choosing a direction almost at random from Zion Square, I walked the length of the Street of the Prophets to come upon a garden courtyard dominated by the circular Abyssinian Church, with a small population of monks and nuns arranging their cloistered lives around it. I was back in another century.

They had planted their Amharic stake here, independent of the Coptic cathedral in the Old City, in recollection of their presumed ancestor, the Queen of Sheba. The place afforded propinquity to the Church of the Holy Sepulchre within the walls and Bethlehem to the south, at that time inaccessible from Israel. The Abyssinians' prayers had proceeded undisturbed by Allenby's expulsion of the Turks in 1917, and on separation from their homeland by Mussolini's conquest of Ethiopia. For them, the most memorable occasion had been a visit from their emperor Haile Selassie, resting a while in his Rehavia villa during his flight from Addis Ababa. One wondered whether they had experienced any echo from the tumults of the Second World War. Every vicissitude had left the pious Abyssinian sectarians unmoved and immovable. They must have been oblivious of the bombing of the King David Hotel by Zionist terrorists in 1946 not to mention the siege of Jerusalem in 1948, when Glubb Pasha's Jordanian Legion almost succeeded in starving the Jews out. Twittering birds lulled my thoughts as I entered the church.

Cool, whitewashed walls bore naive paintings of a symbolism lost on me. Could they relate to those schismatics of ancient Hellenism, in Chalcedon and Antioch? A solicitous custodian began to explain, in French. He might have spared himself. I preferred the silence of the immense rotunda to imagine what it conveyed to such devout Christians in their Jerusalem sanctuary. I felt nearer to Crusades won and lost than to the pressure of today's concerns.

What was it these monks shared with the Jews and their Jerusalem, cherished from afar with their prayers during long Diaspora wanderings? Centuries had elapsed without the Jews themselves building a shrine in Jerusalem, because the Wailing Wall, physical reminder of their Temple, sufficed. But many Hebrew generations had made their final pilgrimage to the Holy City, and reposed on the Mount of Olives, now only to be glimpsed on a crystal clear evening from a King George sidewalk.

That glimpse represented proof positive to some Jews that God had bestowed this ground on them, and only on them. They took the words of the Bible as literal truth, just as other Jews turned the book into a political manifesto. It was all to the same purpose: the restoration of the Holy City once more to an earthly kingdom. Young men and women who coded their intercourse in the private argot of modern Hebrew speech regarded Jerusalem disunited as the sharp end of an Arab spear, poised to slice the Judaean salient from their state. It had almost occurred not half a dozen years earlier. The Arabs could try again. Ben-Gurion was convinced of it.

Such a peril barely equated with the slightest Coptic reality and I left Abyssinian Street to turn into a quarter of entirely different character: no trees to be seen here, nor women either. I found myself in the Street of a Thousand Gates, and the district of that name, Mea Shearim. This was the headquarters of a different war against Zionism, religious and waged without weapons but relentless nevertheless; a war dividing Jew from Jew.

More than a residential quarter, Mea Shearim was a concept – still is, and most probably will continue so until Armageddon. I was now caught in an eighteenth-century time warp, an East European ghetto where no female dared venture without arms and legs fully covered. Save their stockings of white, the men were attired head to toe in black, their sons weedy with faces bleached pale as a winter moon. Most of these proclaimed themselves as disciples of rabbis endowed with near-miraculous gifts, possessors of all the knowledge necessary in man's current incarnation. The rabbis inherited powers passed down dynastically from forebears in Poland and the Ukraine, or perhaps Hungary. An expert could distinguish, from the length of their side-curls and slight variations in their dress (for example, whether the pantaloon trousers beneath their caftans tucked into their stockings at ankle length or were caught up at the knee), which miracle-rabbi they followed.

I penetrated bleak squares, poked my head into little ghetto stores, heard the drone of prayer issuing from stark, ill-lit synagogues. Such was life endured in suspended animation pending the coming of the Messiah, when heaven and earth would join to form another Garden of Eden, all Jewry united in the Holy Land and peace reigning evermore on earth.

In Mea Shearim they hugged a short-term objective too, a yearning for the return of the era of Muslim, not Jewish, temporal authority so that they might cross the frontier to the walled city, and thereby reoccupy unimpeded the traditional Jewish quarter of Jerusalem as it had been in the Ottoman era. This desire to chant their prayers and articulate more personal aspirations (a husband for a daughter perhaps, or a cure for a relation's malady) at the Wailing Wall, hallowed relic of Herod's Temple, controlled their every instinct.

Disturb the arcane practices of these people and you would light a fuse. An automobile advancing upon their territorial preserve on the Sabbath would be ambushed. Not that they contested Christian or Muslim rights in Jerusalem: their political orientation was neutral, even non-existent, except against their modernist fellow-Jews. In this regard they shamed other ultra-fundamentalist fanatics of Zionist ideology, happily few in number, who aspired to tear down the Muslim Dome of the Rock so as to recreate the Temple on its original foundations.

Introspective as they proposed to remain, the followers of the miracle-rabbis were unperturbed by whatever Christian interests existed in this portion of Jerusalem – the Abyssinian church, the picturesque Russian Orthodox Cathedral off the Jaffa Road, Notre Dame of the Catholics, the Greek Orthodox monastery and the newest of them all, St Andrew's Presbyterian church on elevated Abu Tor, memorial to Allenby's fallen and dedicated to Robert the Bruce (I observed St Andrew's minister, in overalls, up a ladder cleaning his windows). But transgression of the strictest rabbinic law, such as mixed bathing in a municipal pool, or advertising some Israeli merchandise by means of a poster turning masculine attention sexwards, would immediately start a riot. The policy of successive Israeli governments is to stay clear of offending the susceptibilities of the 'black hat' inhabitants of Mea Shearim.

I returned to my hotel that afternoon somewhat oppressed

A Very British Subject

in heart. It seemed that this Jerusalem, outwardly so tranquil and for centuries divorced from the normal cares of a metropolis, and which the British in Mandate times described as the city of three Sabbaths and four tomorrows, trembled on a dormant volcano waiting to erupt.

The Eden's foyer, as was usual on a Knesset day, purred contentedly in its clubby atmosphere. Two of the members, to whom I had not so much as been introduced, greeted my appearance with a whisper. One said: 'So you have a meeting with the Old Man today!' And the other: 'Eight o'clock this evening, at B.-G.'s house!'

Evidently they already knew something I didn't. On enquiring at the desk the clerk handed me a note from Navon. Yes, eight o'clock tonight. Was nothing confidential in these parts! Skipping dinner, I went up to my room to collect my thoughts and persuade my empty stomach that its slight turbulence did not register an attack of nerves.

The Prime Minister's official residence, in Rehavia's Ben-Maimon Avenue, was hardly distinguishable from its neighbours to its right and left. In fact it had been the home of a British official, a Manchester Jew killed in the King David explosion. A solitary armed policeman immediately passed me through on hearing the purpose of visit. The story went that Paula Ben-Gurion, who kept no servants, would hold his rifle while she sometimes sent him on an errand at a nearby grocer's.

The great man was seated in his ground floor study, Navon bending over his shoulder. His desk was bare, save for a small notebook into which he scribbled continuously as we talked, like a secretary meticulously taking minutes. The homespun picture of an elderly man in his shirt sleeves put me immediately at ease. Ben-Gurion, man of iron, looked angelic.

Remote and outlandish as it may appear today, one person in London had commanded the world's attention at that time, June 1953. The queen's coronation, occasioning glowing references to the young Elizabeth wherever newspapers circulated, had taken place the day preceding my arrival in Jerusalem.

God's Footstool

Television had not as yet reached Israel, and a sixth sense had advised me to bring copies of the British Press with me. Without ado, Ben-Gurion began by asking about the coronation ceremony. Happily, I withdrew the papers from my briefcase and, walking round to the other side of his desk, spread their pictures before him.

Doubtless the debate as to whether Britain can still afford the luxury of its antique royalty will continue *ad infinitum*, hence one should place that coronation day into the equation. As a public relations exercise the event could have no equal: Westminster Abbey at its glorious best, the solemnity of the majestic hour, the congregation of international personages, the words of the venerable archbishop in blessing the demure young queen and her handsome consort. Those scenes of the old kingdom basking in its quasi-religious aura displaced all other thoughts. And so it was with Ben-Gurion.

'A wonderful young woman', he said, fixing his gaze on the pictures. 'Wonderful.' I received the impression at that moment that Ben-Gurion forgave Britain for the sins, rightly or wrongly, fastened upon its rulers. I interviewed the Prime Minister for an hour. But this was the moment I would most vividly recall.

In truth, the man's personality radiated force. Regard that mass of wiry hair issuing at either side of a head bald to a glaze, the whiteness contrasting with his ruddy complexion, and you could persuade yourself that you were in the presence of an Old Testament prophet. Then 67 and thickened by his years, his voice soft in a sure, heavily-accented English, the man filled a role dedicated to one purpose alone, never foiled by hesitation or dilemma. I had no intention of working through the episodes of his life on this initial discussion, rather to allow him full rein to expatiate on his ideas of what a Jewish State must become. Indeed, no other subject interested him.

Irreligious he might be, but Ben-Gurion knew his Bible, learnt at his father's knee, profoundly. He searched out true history from it, offering the view that the Jews, since their loss of sovereignty in Roman times, had been rendered a nullity, the penalty of their Diaspora existence. They had resumed organised national life again in modern times, with their return to this country as pioneer settlers in the late nineteenth century. Thus he could speak without emotion of Hitler and the European destruction of the people, that cataclysm being the corollary inevitable to their stateless condition; not to be forgotten or forgiven, but a recollection less to be mourned than understood.

Now he indulged his favourite exercise of projecting a future in which Israel would constitute the bridge between East and West. He dismissed those Jews refusing to come and share in the benefits, the privileges and travails of national regeneration as enslaved to their flesh-pots and deprived of the freedom of self-expression. He was obviously pained that hitherto the Diaspora had failed to respond to the message from Jerusalem.

Already well attuned to the high-flown oratory of Zionism, I heard this latter-day Moses out in respectful silence, making my notes. I struggled for a perspective: must he be classed a large fish in a small pond, or truly a man reshaping the destiny of his dispersed people? His achievements, so far Herculean, had solved no problems while creating fresh ones. Israel had crushed an Arab alliance, though peace still remained beyond the horizon, as if the facts on this sacred soil mocked Ben-Gurion's words. It troubled me that I could not reconcile my own sentiments regarding the Jews with Ben-Gurion's. Which of us therefore was the realist, which the dreamer?

It was late evening when I left. Ben-Maimon Avenue, dimly lit, appeared so different now, its houses cubes of gloom where earlier speckled gold bounced off their sandstone frontages. Passers-by threaded in and out of the shadows. I had arranged to meet an acquaintance at the King David Hotel, which was about as close to the Old City as security would allow. The establishment's rear boasted a swimming-pool and terrace that gave off a romantic glow and I envied the animated residents, mostly tourists, busily chattering over their drinks.

Here one was permitted a tantalising view of the walls south

God's Footstool

of the Jaffa Gate and the looming Turkish citadel built into them. What lay behind those stout battlements? Why had Arab and Jew forced themselves into this segregation? The Israelis often warned of a second round, when the Arabs would seek to drive them into the sea. I refused to consider it, but a second round occurred, then a third, whereupon the Israelis breached the Jaffa Gate and seized the lot, making Jerusalem whole. It failed to stop the warfare. What could?

The Zionists, obsessed with 'normalising' the Jewish people, saw themselves as Europeans. Thus their attitude of arrogance towards the Arabs, their ignorance of the passions inherent to Islam, their complacency in the superiority of the western way of life and their relegation of Oriental Sephardic Jews to a lower category described as 'Levantinism'. The King David Hotel stood directly opposite an equally imposing edifice likewise constructed with western money: the YMCA. The architectural symbols favoured by both buildings deferred to a Jerusalem of three religions and cultures. Still, they made conflicting statements. The hotel exuded opulence and privilege and authority. It faced the West. The YMCA reminded those patronising it of unfinished business. Its slender tower gazed eastward, into the Valley of Kidron, then distantly to Jericho where a refugee camp would produce a generation yet unborn to continue its parents' struggle. No one forgets Jerusalem.

The next time I saw Ben-Gurion it was to hear him address the Knesset. There was not an empty place in the chamber. Never once was his long speech interrupted, every member being on his best behaviour. His *tour d'horizon* took in a passage from Ezekiel, an affectionate reference to America's previous president Harry Truman, the contemplated repopulation of the Negev desert, the urgency to build a major port at Ashdod as alternative to Haifa. His final words were in glorification of the Hebrew language, about whose syntax Ben-Gurion termed himself a pedant.

What would have become of this man, I asked myself, had he joined the great stream of his contemporaries crossing the Atlantic when he decided to go with a trickle of Jews in the

A Very British Subject

opposite direction? Arguably, just one more garment manufacturer on Seventh Avenue. I pictured Rosetti awaiting his pension amid the files of Stepney Borough Council, and recalled a man I knew as a sergeant in the British army, but now a general in Israel. The magic of new-born statehood!

Eventually my biography was completed. Before its publication I despatched the galley proofs to Ben-Gurion, who by this time had gone temporarily to earth and joined a kibbutz deep in the Negev desert. In reply he sent me his observations in a handwritten letter of 40 notebook pages divided in three envelopes, each addressed in that same meticulous hand.

'When I first heard that you wanted to write a life without knowing Hebrew', Ben-Gurion wrote, 'it seemed to me an impossible undertaking. Now reading through the proofs I was astonished to see that you did it . . . I don't assume that you yourself believe it is perfect, nor do I consider it a failure.'

Frequently returning to Jerusalem in later years, I would be able to cross the walls through the Damascus Gate into the bustling *souk*, where the Armenian shopkeepers offered souvenirs to suit all religious preferences. I would slip off my shoes to enter the Mosque of Omar, with the rock where Abraham was tested to sacrifice his son Isaac, then change the Muslim scene for a Christian shrine by boarding a bus to Bethlehem. On the modern side of Jerusalem tourism, whore that it is, would take its toll, and the gaps between the buildings of King George would fill with hotels of Hiltonian ostentation. A rainy day would bring traffic chaos warranting a description by Dante.

Jerusalem grew, suburb upon suburb, and though many new buildings would merit architectural laurels, they covered the tradition-steeped western corridor to the coast with concrete. So Israel was now definitely and irrevocably established? You might say that. However, many Israelis have now emigrated, especially to America, where they possess their own Hebrew radio station and newspaper in New York. Garment manufacturers they may not become, yet the Diaspora retains its lure nevertheless, even reaching to Jerusalem.

12 • One Danubian Summer

Now that the Cold War has fizzled into a rubbish heap of nuclear weapons unfired, and in a renewal of nineteenth-century ethnic disputes, we contemplate that old Iron Curtain with a tinge of nostalgia. Europe had simplified as a continent of Us and Them. On the one hand the situation nourished our western self-esteem. On the other it quickened our curiosity about cities whose inhabitants tamely queued all hours for a kilo of sausage, while a motor car could be parked in a main street without incurring those penalties of capitalism, clamped wheels and traffic jams.

Nostalgia requires a mood to ride in tandem. Once past the age of 50, a person so inclined may slip into wistfulness as he scans the globe, in the likelihood that he will never live to see large areas of it. Fifty constitutes a benchmark when there is more to be relished looking backward than anticipated ahead. My half-century approached with Europe still divided by its infamous curtain, so-called, and I worried lest I would be denied a vision of that other half. Calcutta and Tokyo could happily wait. That part of the world was not going to melt away. In time my economic prospects would bring them within reach, to be conquered in one swoop along with Australasia. The Communist bloc was different. It might well transmogrify one day into package-tour country covered with invitations to try the local fish and chips.

Eastern Europe was not exactly closed against the West. One encountered privileged travellers parading intimate knowledge of Moscow, or Prague, or Warsaw before an envious audience. Khrushchev then initiated a thaw. He allowed a certain freedom of movement, cultural exchanges and a sprinkling of adventurous strangers. Intourist maintained a bureau in Regent Street, and though its window displays were hardly encouraging, they attracted customers who emerged triumphantly with bookings for Tashkent and Alma Ata. Why should I delay?

We are, all of us, the exception to some rule. In my case this took the form of refusal of a visa. My application was not for the purpose of giving a lecture, or shepherding a school party, or organising a group visit to the Bolshoi Ballet. Had any of these applied, my passport would doubtless have been swiftly stamped by an official with the welcoming cry *dobro pozhalovat*! on his lips. However, Khrushchev had gone to his eternal Soviet. The era now belonged to Brezhnev. An ice age threatened. In 1971 I wished to visit the USSR as a mere tourist. This created a slight problem: they didn't believe me.

My intention was to drive with my family across Europe to Leningrad and Moscow, then south to visit Odessa, where both my parents and those of my wife Sylvia had originated. We could not think of going to Russia without a pilgrimage to our roots in the Ukraine. Our itinerary was agreed, hotels were alerted, motor car prepared for the long haul. But instead of a visa I was invited with my wife for an interview with the Soviet Consul-General in London.

He was a friendly bureaucrat with a Lithuanian name (he emphasised this) and greeted us cordially enough. Across the years we in the West had suspected every interview with a Russian to be secretly taped, and every official a KGB agent in masquerade. Sylvia and I felt we had entered the lion's den. A coffee-pot bubbled away on a corner table, so it was easy for me to convince myself that it concealed some device to take my picture, record my political views and ultimately put me in the dreaded Lubyanka. I suspected possible complications because for some years a Jewish campaign had mounted for Russia to permit its Jews to emigrate to Israel. I could easily be part of that sinister international conspiracy.

Indeed, this was the trouble. The Soviet Union was not keen to allow Jewish writers into the country, since they would surely be in search of material to fuel the agitation. Some Jews had visited proclaiming innocence in this regard, only to be discovered distributing prayer books and Zionist leaflets. Disturbances had ensued.

'Why', the Consul-General asked, 'do you intend a visit to Odessa?' I explained. Our parents had spoken of their native city frequently, and it would be an act of reverence for their memory besides sheer curiosity. He agreed, but then added: 'And you will write something, an article or a book, afterwards?'

I assured him to the contrary. Even writers take holidays. We would be accompanied by our two sons. I requested no Press facilities, though conceded that he probably would not believe me.

'On the contrary', he replied amiably. 'I do believe you. I am quite good at making judgements on people. But you will meet other Jews over there?'

'Of course, should I encounter any. That would be natural.'

'And you are a Zionist?'

'What Jew can persuade himself that he is not a Zionist? It is an instinct.'

He thought about this. Then declared: 'If it were not for Stalin you might not have had Israel. He pushed the United Nations. My country was the very first to recognise Israel, hours before America.' I allowed the observation to pass.

The Consul-General decided he would let us know in due course, after consulting Moscow. It did not strike me as strange at the time, but our interview was twice interrupted, first by a British gentleman introduced to me as a Jewish banker, then by a Russian professor, also Jewish, of Moscow University. Had they arrived deliberately to look us over and, in the case of the Londoner, perhaps to recognise me as a likely trouble-maker?

I would never know, though another episode served to complicate the situation somewhat. The Consul-General asked for copies of my books, which he would send to Moscow for examination. Sylvia volunteered to bring them, and by chance turned up at the door of the Consulate at the precise moment it was locked against a siege by a group of students demonstrating against Soviet policy regarding the Jews. My wife rang the bell nevertheless. The door opened a crack and she explained her errand. This gained her entry and an opportunity for the students to swarm in, as if taking possession. Scuffles resulted. On the whole the outlook for our visit to Russia was none too auspicious.

Not hearing from the Consul-General during the following three weeks, by which time our impatient sons embarked on holidays with other companions elsewhere, I presumed the visas were refused. Out came the atlas of Europe again. We decided on a near alternative to Russia, with a tour of Hungary and Romania, both of them in the Communist orbit and, in 1971, still beyond the radius of Britain's holiday-seeking public. Enquiries quickly became plans. The Consul-General of the Soviet Union then telephoned a message replete, he suggested, with good cheer.

'Your visas are granted', he stated. 'You will travel by air, joining a group visiting Leningrad and Moscow.' Evidently the package deal, Benidorm style, was about to break over Russia.

'Not separately, in our motor car?'

'No, I am sorry.'

'And not Odessa?'

'It is not on the itinerary.'

I thanked him but declined the invitation. It thus happened, through frustration, that we embarked upon an exploration of the two Communist countries sharing between them a large part of the lower reaches of the Danube. In the present era of open frontiers it hardly catches the imagination as a journey into the unknown. At that time, for us, it approached adventure. Our first halt would be Vienna, to meet our old friends the Sponsiks. Any meeting with them inevitably turned into an adventure.

Herbert and Jessie Sponsik met as students in their home

town of St Louis, Missouri, where they attended medical school. Jessie eventually graduated as a physician, though never practised. While a medical student Herbert aspired to become a professional singer, but the money ran out without his fulfilment in either vocation and, ever adaptable, he turned his skills to salesmanship. He traded in hospital equipment throughout the Middle West, where apparently the pickings were easy for those intent upon riches. This was not Herbert's way, for at the age of 50 he calculated that, by living frugally, he and Jessie could raise their two daughters reasonably enough without their having ever to work again.

Not unusually for Americans, the Sponsiks decided to enrol themselves into the life of middle-class gypsies all round the world, but particularly in Europe to ensure the propriety of their children's education. Those two girls were just rough-cut Missouri teenage hicks, though by the time they fled the embarrassment of being the Sponsiks' daughters, and made decisions of solid work and more conventional goals for themselves, they were part of an international fraternity of young sophisticates. At home in almost every major city of Western Europe, they spoke French and Italian as fluently as English, finally to make the best of marriages in Los Angeles. The parents continued their roaming still, fortunate enough through their modest independent income to do so untrammelled while eternally marvelling at their daughters' entrenchment among the élite of America's Pacific coast.

Vienna was by no means a prosperous city in 1971, yet Herbert drove what surely must have been the most decrepit vehicle in the Austrian capital. Happily, he knew about motor cars just as he understood the mysteries of domestic plumbing and was adept at renewing a garden fence. Herbert wandered through hardware stores like an academic browsing in a library. I used to save all necessary repairs around my house for his periodic visits to London. He would arrive with a pocket full of nails and a screwdriver and spirit level at the ready in his luggage.

The car he drove in Vienna had been through several hands

in brutal service the length and breadth of Europe. Occasionally it gave out on the road, when Herbert, none too disconcerted, withdrew a heavy spanner from his tool-box and, treating the poor thing like an obstinate mule, struck it sharply on the bonnet. Whereupon the jalopy struggled on for another few miles without demur. It was in this vehicle that Herbert invited us to join them for an excursion to Bratislava, capital of Slovakia. It would be our initiation into socialist society as pursued along the Danube. Sylvia and I could not resist.

Though not in Herbert's car. We took our own, and not only because of the hazards of transportation the Sponsik way. There also loomed the Jessie factor. A wonderful companion taken in small doses, she was otherwise an endurance test. She talked incessantly, mainly about food, and always insisted upon speaking through a phrase book to the locals in their native language, whatever the country. The result invariably proved the reverse of communication.

Missouri likes to describe itself as the Show Me State, and Jessie carried the motto everywhere on her extraordinary travels. She needed to see everything, meet all the people, sample their speciality dishes and retail the total experience to Herbert in a loud voice as though from a distance and against competition. And this despite his very rare absence from her side. As a trained doctor, and an American, Jessie travelled with a small portmanteau of tablets, drugs and lotions. They enabled her to maintain a close check on her husband's health. Principally, she was concerned in breaking his smoking habit, an activity in which she largely failed.

Normally it is no great problem to drive from Vienna to Bratislava. They are a mere 30 miles apart and we proposed making an afternoon of it. In pleasurable anticipation we reached the frontier without mishap and obtained permits to enter Czechoslovakia in minutes. The formalities included a requirement to change a minimum amount of money. The equivalent of five pounds produced a large quantity of Czechoslovak crowns in paper currency, to be spent entirely within the country or be confiscated on departure.

Herbert's motor car, however, aroused the suspicions of the customs officials. It simply did not match his United States passport. They knew the famous Detroit marques, which in those days still proclaimed quality and brought a swallow to European throats by their size. This automobile, however, already limping on the approach to the check-point as if reluctant to cross the great divide, gave no indication of mighty transatlantic power – more a botched together example of uninspired improvisation. It bore no recognisable design and apparently preferred anonymity, for it shied from displaying a maker's badge.

While our own Triumph passed muster after a casual glance into our open boot, Herbert's vehicle was subjected to thorough examination, engine, glove compartment and underside included. Where did he buy it? Its documentation was over-stamped so many times it told too many tales. (Herbert had acquired it at a bargain price sight unseen from a departing journalist at some obscure Mediterranean port.) Unfortunately, he stood dumb while Jessie did all the talking, adding complications to the interrogation. She tried to describe the vehicle's provenance, and explain how it was intended only to serve them during their sojourn in Vienna, which was due to be brief. Fully an hour of our afternoon disappeared in the process.

At length a police officer, obviously against his better judgement, waved the Sponsiks into Czechoslovakia, and Bratislava appeared a few hundred yards from the frontier. A city with a long, chequered history, it looked its age – rather grey, very quiet. In walking the streets we encountered few young people. An elderly man steering a loaded barrow observed the quartet of strangers and greeted us in English. He had recently returned from Baltimore, he informed us, where his daughter resided, but decided to return to this country to protect his pension and housing rights. 'Baltimore or Bratislava, what's the difference?' he asked in a raised voice. Having myself visited Baltimore, I could understand the question.

The man pointed out Bratislava Castle as perhaps deserving

an inspection, hardly a compelling recommendation. Herbert and Jessie were beyond the age when they readily scaled hills, and with the afternoon rapidly ebbing we decided to give the castle a miss. Instead, we chose to patronise a coffee house with a rack of foreign newspapers, the one in English being the *Morning Star*.

Gloom pervaded this town, Czechoslovakia's second city, possibly attributable to a malaise following the heroic 'Prague Spring' of 1968 and the consciousness of Brezhnev's long arm. The removal by the police of a drunk creating a nuisance in the main square attracted quite a crowd, evidently grateful for any diversion. By this time Jessie evinced some anxiety lest we leave the country without making purchases sufficient to consume our quota of the national currency. Though a down-market shopper, Jessie was a relentless one.

In the square – formerly named in honour of Josef Stalin though now commemorating the 1944 Slovak revolt against the Nazis – a large clothing store beckoned attention. My wife had long concluded that I needed a new pair of shorts, the khaki version rather than the dinky whites in which men had begun to disport themselves along the Riviera. I was addicted to the khaki, but in Britain they had become a rarity, even in army surplus retailers (at least, until Marks and Spencer rendered them a women's fashion by describing them as 'culottes'). There was no mistaking this store as an official government emporium, since it could have been the domain of a British quartermaster in a large military depot.

I explained my requirement with a gesture that in other circumstances would be considered obscene, and was directed by a managerial person to a saleswoman behind a wide barrier of a counter. Looking me over, she understood my quest and produced a pair of shorts for my examination. They appeared the correct size and I nodded contentedly, whereupon the saleswoman snatched the garment back. She then filled in a complicated form in triplicate, handing me two copies. Thus fortified, I joined a queue, and eventually passed the copies with money over to an assistant framed at an open window. A rubber stamp plunged down to seal the legality of the transaction. In exchange for one copy of the receipt I received my shorts, of such sterling quality I wear them to this day. In the meanwhile Jessie Sponsik had seen nothing in the store to tempt her.

The Danube is attractively set off at Bratislava by St Martin's Cathedral, where for over 200 years Hungarian kings had come to be crowned. We were denied entry, however, as extensive renovation was in progress. But in the cathedral shadows private enterprise reigned in the form of stall-holders offering fruit and vegetables. This was a category of merchandise meriting Jessie's attention. A strange ritual was thereupon enacted.

Jessie began carefully choosing apples one by one and placing them on the scales. As she picked, the lady vendor retrieved the apples and restored them to her pile. Jessie affected not to notice, and continued to make her choice. The lady took them back. Rhythmically, the hands worked around each other, an action worthy of musical accompaniment. The rest of us grew a trifle embarrassed, Herbert particularly, for he discreetly walked away. Suddenly the stall-holder mouthed a most dismissive sound, placed stout protective arms over her apples and indicated to Jessie that she should take her custom elsewhere. The concept of 'pick 'n mix' still awaited its introduction in Slovakia.

By now we were due to head back to Vienna, in the guilty knowledge that we had treated Bratislava shabbily by such an abbreviated stay. But where was Jessie? She had gone off shopping on her own. 'How did you use up your currency?' I enquired when she caught us up. 'There's absolutely nothing worth buying in this place', she said morosely, 'so I was forced to use up their money in cigarettes for Herbert.'

Vienna meant the parting of the ways, ourselves to Hungary, the Sponsiks to ditch their automobile and fly off for recuperation in Los Angeles. They were each past 60 years of age by then, still pacing their resources to enable them to linger wherever the mood took them. Herbert retained his fine baritone and between long silences enjoyed bursting into medleys that included opera, light music and traditional ballads. His fetching humility concealed a wise head and a touching optimism. She it was who planned the trips, organised their accommodation and made the world their friend. They had formerly spent a year in England with their children, taking a modest house in a North London suburb for a base so as to keep expenses on a tight rein. It formed part of a long terrace of houses where neighbours passed each other regularly in the street without coming closer than to bid a polite good morning. Jessie changed all that. She invited them home in groups to get acquainted, so that before the Sponsiks departed the terrace of closed front doors was transformed into a warm community. We wondered whether we would meet again, but it happened, frequently, on both sides of the Atlantic. The association continues through the generations to our grandchildren.

It was early in August when we left Vienna, Sylvia driving and I reading the maps. Hungarian frontier formalities offered no difficulties and our route took us to a town we had not previously heard of, with a name, Szombathely, we couldn't then pronounce. Here again we were assailed by that eerie stillness perceived in Bratislava, though accentuated by the extreme heat. Roman ruins and a museum devoted to the realism of proletarian art evidently attracted few visitors. Our hotel, one of those soulless geometric structures that poor cities erect in the hope of becoming noticed, gave off an atmosphere of enthusiasm defeated, an edifice conscious of being in the wrong place. Apparently the entire Hungarian population were holiday-making on Lake Balaton, which we had decided to avoid.

The hotel occupied one corner of a square with room for a hundred cars – that is, until we decided to park there. A policeman promptly materialised and ordered us off. I pointed to a stationary cluster of black Russian Zis limousines invariably associated in the West with Communist officials of the highest privileged echelons (rightly so, it transpired) and declined to move. This, my earliest defiance of the *nomenklatura*, proved a victory. Henceforward I treated the régime cavalierly whenever I deemed it appropriate, and was not once threatened with deportation, incarceration or beheading.

An insignificant Hungarian town of this isolated region was no place for an extended stay. Enough that our reflexes had absorbed the abrupt transition from the irrepressible gaiety of the Viennese to the dour taciturnity of the Magyars, and the drop from abundance to scarcity. We noted how the locals advertised their yearning for western delights by consuming vast quantities of Coca Cola, even at breakfast, and departed. Next stop, Budapest.

Exhausting as the hundred-mile drive proved, for Szombathely did not at that time connect with Budapest by a major road, we quite enjoyed getting lost in a big city where few people had hitherto seen a car with a GB plate. We felt important. Those with a modicum of English were keen to direct us to the Aero Hotel, though initially we could find no one who had heard of it. And no wonder: it was not marked on a street guide, being newly built and remote from the city centre. The planners had located the hotel, as its name implied, to serve the airport. Its magnitude would have done justice to the monsters crowding each other off the Costa Brava. No matter. We thoroughly appreciated the delicious evening meal provided – caviare, chicken expertly roasted, peach melba and a good wine.

Another pleasant surprise awaited us in the lounge immediately afterwards. We were being officially welcomed by the Hungarian Travel Bureau.

'I am Margot', announced the stately lady as she approached with the step of a grenadier and an expression informed with the solemnity of a representative conducting high affairs on behalf of the People's Republic of Hungary. 'Here is your programme.' From her handbag, the size of a filing cabinet, she excavated a typewritten sheet. 'You will see what is included in the price and all other possibilities. This evening we have the "By Night". Eleven dollars. You will enjoy.'

Cowed by the representative's authoritarian personality, and fatigued by the long day's bumping over a secondary road, we accepted the 'By Night' against our better judgement. 'The wine tasting, the night life and the Hungarian folk-dancing', Margot told us. 'Your guide will be here at ten o'clock.'

We materialised as an international group of six: an American couple, a German couple and ourselves, the guide doubling as minibus driver. Conviviality was contributed by the guide alone, as the rest had little desire, nor felt any obligation, to exchange pleasantries. The women addressed their partners from time to time in whispers. It was as if we were challenging Budapest, whose various landmarks were pointed out, to keep us entertained. Budapest tried, without success.

'By night', Margot had promised, eyes flashing. And so it transpired: a dreary round of hotels, backed by a cacophony of so-called gypsy music. Tourism in Hungary emerged as a labour-intensive industry to a substantial degree. The wine tasting consisted of a single glass of Tokay so elaborately served it involved the attendance of three waiters for our table. Once emptied, the glasses were whisked away and replaced in time for the waiters to return and thrust new bottles under our noses. A supplementary charge was of course extorted, escape for the innocents being out of the question. Musicians hovered with their violins at our table while their leader treated us to individual serenades, starting with me. The enclosed atmosphere, the perspiration of the formally dressed musicians, the nearness of the leader's instrument to my chin, combined to create an almost unendurable pressure. He continued nevertheless, as though awaiting my command before withdrawing.

A fellow-reveller, the quiet American from whom there had not hitherto issued a sound, indicated how I could put myself out of my misery. 'He won't stop until you give him a tip', he muttered, evidently an old hand at the By Night routine. I placed a coin beside my glass, and sure enough the violinist moved up the line. Our companions learned from my ordeal. No sooner had the bow descended for the first bar of music than the money appeared, and he relented. What most interested Sylvia and me in this country, breeding ground of Bartók and Kodály, was the musicians' conception of Hungarian gypsy music. It appeared to consist of variations on a theme long ago laid to rest in Britain, *Roll out the Barrel*. Altogether an exhausting night, which did not conclude until 2 am, when mercifully we were delivered back to the Aero Hotel.

Just as I was dropping off to sleep Sylvia murmured: 'What about the floor show with folk-dancing exhibition, according to the programme Margot gave us?' Ah, had we been robbed? I taxed Margot, again in attendance the following evening, with a gentle reproach. She was more than equal to the challenge. 'That was the 18 dollar By Night. You chose the other one.' Conclusion of discussion.

Budapest revealed its better nature and a much more likeable face when, guide-book in hand, we engaged in sight-seeing on our own account. At last, the bustle of real people in a city graciously rising from the Buda bank of the Danube. And not a tower block in sight. I searched to no avail for signs of that old *belle époque* when Budapest showed the rest of Europe how to relax, producing film-makers, composers, brilliant journalists. Vienna had first sucked out the best of them, whereupon America gathered up the rest (lucky Hollywood!). Hungary was ever fated to choose the wrong side in war and was reduced to a remnant of its extent in 1914. Budapest, on our visit, had lost the sinews of a metropolis.

The general absence of foreigners granted us the distinction of being travellers rather than tourists. The only foreign cars to be seen bore Polish and German number plates. We rarely experienced difficulty in making ourselves understood, for simple English can be fairly easily acquired, and many Hungarians tried their tongues out on it. The Englishman they knew best was old Lord Rothermere, who championed their cause in his newspapers after the First World War and was once offered the royal crown. A curious blend of collectivisation and private enterprise, happier by-product of the Hungarian uprising of 1956, enabled the industrious to work in a government factory yet take lots of time off to keep a bookstall perhaps, or run a store selling musical instruments and sheet music, even a restaurant or florist's, and make good money on the side.

The government restaurants proved a real discovery. There was no mistaking them, fancy names rejected for the simple word *etterin*, restaurant. They offered a wholesome bowl of soup thick with meat for a negligible sum. Patrons had no choice, except that vegetarians could take a meatless dish, while those producing the appropriate medical certificate were entitled to their individual diet. We stood at high circular counters and traffic was heavy. Whatever happened to our famous 'British Restaurants' developed during the war? Presumably this Hungarian version will go the same way once fast food 'eateries' spread themselves over the East. Where Coca Cola has conquered could McDonald's be far behind?

Buda, as one would expect, is dominated 200 feet up by the palace on Castle Hill. The edifice started as a fortress to hold back the Mongols, and was subsequently endowed with Gothic embellishment to shelter warrior kings, after which the Turks took possession while converting every nearby church into a mosque. The Ottoman retreat of the seventeenth century left the place in dereliction, until Habsburg emperors set about its revival and splendification. Then Kossuth, the national hero, returned the palace, albeit briefly, to the Hungarians. It remained as a monument to Magyar sentiment for another hundred years, when Hitler's army fortified it in preparation for Budapest's unsuccessful stand against the Red Army.

Sylvia and I, our feet protesting, traipsed through a dozen rooms. The castle had been afflicted by fire, brutalised by neglect, turned into stables for the convenience of proud cavalry regiments, cleansed and renovated a score of times. We now observed that Communism was extracting the ultimate sacrifice by turning the palace into a shrine to the virtues of proletarian man.

During the castle tour we spoke with a Hungarian visitor

who, if typical, indicated that patriotism was still very much alive in his country. He referred with bitterness to those large numbers who, following the uprising of 1956 and the momentary opening of the frontiers, had abandoned their homeland before the Russians came in to reseal the border. The worst of the expatriates in his estimation were those now returning in their new personae as American tourists and flaunting their prosperity in glittering automobiles.

'Life is hard here', the Hungarian admitted. 'To make a living I have to hold down two jobs. But it's getting better all the time.' Then he smiled. 'You also have problems. Protestants and Catholics don't go about killing each other in Hungary, but look at Ireland! You left us to Russia's mercy in 1956.'

By the morning of our third day we had strolled across the bridges linking Buda with Pest and back again half a dozen times besides enjoying an hour's trip on the Danube for the equivalent of a shilling, and felt in tune with the city. One quickly formed an affection for a people so polite, and so curious about the world beyond, which few of them expected ever to see. It was with regret that we took to the road again. All our hotels were pre-booked and any effort to change them likened to an exercise in reversing night and day.

Our next destination, Salgotarjan, was a town described in the publicity brochure as possessing 'many fine speciments [*sic*] of the socialist building activity' – magnetic words. For us its interest lay in Salgotarjan's location in the hilly region of the Palots, people claiming descent from pagan tribes of dim antiquity. To judge from posters in the tourist bureau, the Palots country folk regularly attired themselves in colourful native costume, displayed their local crafts and indulged their passion for folk dancing. Ostensibly their cultural festivals were famous world wide. Approaching the mountainous terrain, castle ruins again testified to dogged protestations against successive invasions, though not once did we encounter a Palots person rigged out in clothes that would appear extraordinary in Stockton-on-Tees.

A Very British Subject

They had routed us to Salgotarjan for easy access to Hollokó, a village where, according to Margot's programme, a festival of folk art would be in progress to which we received an official invitation. We were dubious about taking the journey deep into the hills, given the hazards of Hungary's minor roads. This would be a minor road indeed. Hollokó did not exist on any map in our possession. The hotel clerk drew a rough sketch.

Anticipating colourful bunting, cottages bedecked with flowers and the usual exhibition of local handicrafts, we reached Hollokó after an hour's snailing drive. The only life in evidence was three ducks in the village pond. A medieval, timbered church stood locked and barred against all comers. Sylvia applied the brakes and leaned on the Triumph's steering-wheel. What to do now? Her tone registered an accusation of my incompetence. Then we actually saw a human being. 'The festival?' I called out, not knowing what else to say.

The villager looked puzzled, but gestured towards a simple cottage some yards away. What to enquire for there, and how to describe ourselves, I hadn't the slightest idea. Nevertheless I tapped on the door. The shirt-sleeved young man who emerged seemed taken aback a trifle. Greeting us in Hungarian, he scrutinised the car. Ah, tourists. The young man bowed a friendly *'guten Abend'*. So communication was feasible. 'Folklore programme?' I asked. He was full of apologies. It had been cancelled weeks ago.

This proved, however, to be the liveliest encounter of our entire trip. The man's wife appeared. She ushered us in, gave us coffee, showed us their two young children, unearthed a midget German-Hungarian dictionary, and all became light. Husband and wife were the village schoolteachers, doubtless also the local historians and folklore specialists, while we turned out to be the first English people they had ever encountered in the flesh. Apparently no visitors had arrived for many a week before us.

He was Mihaelik, she Christine. Their home consisted of two rooms and an attic from which Christine brought down a photograph album. A bottle of wine came with it, and we leafed through the album to observe the development of their two children, now four and six, from birth to the present. They deeply regretted we could not inspect the House of Culture and glass works of Hollokó, but both were closed for the summer. We threw them an appropriate glance of frustration at the news. Sylvia and Christine then began struggling through an interchange of domestic rituals in their respective civilisations. Mihaelik had more ambitious plans for me – an exploration of the fortress ruin round which the village had grown.

The fortress was destined one day to become a number one tourist attraction, he explained. They were awaiting a government grant to render it safe for visitors. However, there was no good reason why we should not carefully pick our way through the stones now and enjoy the view from the top. Dutifully I agreed, and soon realised that acquiescence involved gambling with my life.

Mihaelik led me across narrow planks positioned to bridge deep chasms between slippery rock and damaged brickwork, then we climbed and climbed, my head swimming. By this time I feared the challenge of going forward but shrank from the perils of descent, while he, swift as a young antelope, held himself fastened with one hand and extended the other to me. Thus we continued, seeking precarious footholds over sheer parapets, British honour compelling me on, to the summit. He pointed towards the Czechoslovak frontier and waved away imaginary Turks who had besieged the fortress centuries ago. The downward slide occupied us until twilight, with an anxious Sylvia awaiting our return far below.

It was more than time for us to find our way back to Salgotarjan, and I, still somewhat light in the head, was determined to drive. Mihaelik would have none of it. I had proved myself a *ferfias*, he repeated, whatever the term might mean (a truly manly man, it transpired). My reward would be a visit to the village bar, for a *ferfias* drink. Pálinka, he said, for such a hero. The women remained behind while Mihaelik dragged me to the barn-like hostelry, evidently an exclusively male preserve. The pálinka, a potent apricot brandy, was produced, and my stomach sensed trouble. Toasts were drunk to both our countries, with the company joining in. Every Englishman is a patriot abroad, and I laboured hard in defence of my side's reputation.

I could barely totter my way back to the car. Sylvia, clutching her own gift, a doll in traditional Palots dress, virtually sprang to the wheel at sight of me. The farewells at last done, darkness fell. The road required skill of the utmost in navigation, myself hanging from the Triumph's door and depositing the contents of my stomach along the route. That night passed miserably for the conqueror of the Hollokó fortress. Needless to say, we declined an invitation next morning to visit Salgotarjan's two showpieces: the underground mining museum and the Institute of the Working Class Movement.

I vowed not to touch another drop of alcohol in Hungary, but this was not the resolution to make in Miskolc, our next port of call in the extreme north-east of the country. Avas Hill rises out of the very loins of Miskolc, and has been used for centuries for the regional storage of wine. The cellars bore deep into the hill all round its lower reaches. In our climb, which we undertook without ado so as to get it over, we trod a soil concealing thousands of bottles of Tokay, both sweet and dry, and so cheap by the glass it would strain the self-discipline of a saint.

Our Victorian hotel, we decided, made a refreshing change after the stereotyped accommodation so far provided, all in studied emulation of the worst endeavours blighting the West. It was a contrast indeed. Victorian also implied decrepit – cracked ceilings, peeling wallpaper, a bathroom tap producing brown liquid, and so close to the traffic in the narrow main street we could see the passengers in the rattling tramcars from our room. Miskolc, the guidebook wrote, was a thriving industrial centre. In fact it did strike me as a city full of life, pleased with itself and boasting a medieval castle containing a room dedicated to a nineteenth-century actress called Mrs Very.

Apparently the toast of the Austro-Hungarian Empire, her final performance (a dramatic death) occurred here in Miskolc.

Having visited the two Gothic churches, Orthodox and Calvinist, we felt the need to restore spiritual balance and pay respect to a synagogue. Hungary has many of them, for the large part unused and neglected, testifying, like everywhere else in Eastern Europe, to congregations of ghosts. The few Jews surviving the Hitler period had mostly taken whatever opportunities were offered to emigrate. That Friday evening we attended service at the only Miskolc synagogue still functioning. A dozen or so elderly men and women present emphasised the superfluity of the great building. The beadle, approaching with obvious relief, welcomed us. Only nine men were among them till I arrived, so I completed the *minyan* (quorum) of ten necessary for collective prayers; not that I was required to participate, just being there satisfied the rules. The women, Sylvia among them, were seated separately, since they were not counted as valid members of the congregation.

Following the service we all assembled in the rabbi's study for coffee, women included. We talked, and the beadle very proudly brought out a photograph. It was of his son, a soldier in uniform guarding Israel's borders. 'Hungarians are not permitted to emigrate', the beadle told us, 'and I sent him away as a boy to relatives when the frontiers opened during the uprising. Hungary has no diplomatic contact with Israel. He cannot come here on a visit.'

'So you haven't seen your son since 1956?'

'We meet every year in Romania. We are allowed to travel within the socialist bloc only. Romania still maintains relations with Israel, and that's where we arrange reunions with our Israeli families. One day perhaps God will grant that I join my son over there.'

Jewish life in this country, where a population of over half a million flourished before the Second World War in all branches of society, was evidently whimpering to extinction. Here in Miskolc a mere handful remained, refusing to admit that the Jewish God had abandoned them. For surely the

Omniscient One would have known the Holocaust would occur, as he would have advance knowledge of the assassination of President Kennedy, the massacre at Tiananman Square, and who would win the World Cup? If a believer, you must believe he transcends time and space, summoning you to prayer not for the purpose of debating with him, but to understand. These few at Miskolc, isolated in a country itself isolated, must therefore have understood. Uncomplainingly they met once every week on the Sabbath Eve, solely for the privilege of being in his presence. We shook hands with them all before parting – except for the rabbi, who refused Sylvia's hand when she extended it. A man so deep in his faith would touch no woman save his own wife.

Back in the material world, we proceeded to Debrecen via Lillafüred, celebrated for its spectacular waterfall; but summer's heat had dried up the gorge. Among our possessions were vouchers for lunch at Tokay, the village of vineyards, including a bottle of its famous *cru*. The restaurant overlooked the river Tisza, and therefore this hospitality, included among the extras thrown in with Hungary's compliments, was not to be despised. Nevertheless, we found ourselves wondering whether our vouchers would incur incomprehension, as with the non-existent folklore festival at Hollokó.

All went without a hitch, despite the risk of consuming too much wine against the continuation of motoring under that merciless midday sun. And this after my solemn pledge to abstain. We chose a main course blindly, recognising only the word 'paprika'. Happily, it proved a most appetising dish, yellow peppers stuffed with beef and rice, the whole dressed in a pure tomato sauce. Entering Debrecen like the advance party of a conquering army, spirits high, we took up residence at the Hotel Arany Bika (the 'Golden Bull') in the central square. A walk along the major thoroughfare still going by the designation Red Army Road found us near the gateway of the Puszta, Hungary's great plain.

It comprises a thousand square miles of featureless steppe, immediately accessible by car out of Debrecen on route 33. At

One Danubian Summer

this writing I recall the immortal words of President Nixon on being introduced to the Great Wall of China. 'That's a great wall', declared Nixon, precisely as I reacted to the great plain of Hungary: 'What a great plain!' Without a compass an innocent British traveller could undoubtedly meet his end there. We had no compass. All credit, therefore, to the Hungarians for maintaining the region in its virginity as a spatial monument to the Golden Horde of unlamented memory.

Horse and cattle breeding, rice fields and fish ponds are situated at various points, if one can find them. We travelled for some 45 lifeless miles, when discretion warned us to make for a group of habitations and venture no further. The settlement, known as Hortobagy, possessed facilities for light refreshment and refuelling, together with a photographic exhibition devoted to the lore of the Puszta and its cattle-breeding traditions. The tuning up of an orchestra in the little restaurant signalled that our return to Debrecen should not be delayed a moment longer.

Since the crashing of the Berlin Wall in 1989 and the consequent elimination of the European divide, too much is in the process of change to chance any pontification on the Hungarian national character, least of all after a brief holiday visit. We observed a people obviously proud of their ethnic singularity though without pomposity. If they resented their enclosure within the Soviet orbit they revealed no sign. Evidence of the austere egalitarian paradise existed everywhere – in the shops, in the general earnestness of the people, in the rudimentary dwellings we passed in our progress around the country.

Who was to say they were not happy? That's the wrong question. Better, were they a people living in fear and restless for change? I could not tell. Many of Britain's citizens yearn for change, enough to judge our country, in the eyes of some outsiders, as ripe for revolution. We, of course, possess the freedom to voice discontent. The Hungarians covered their feelings with a blanket of solemnity, which is silent. We would soon be made aware of the contrast with Romania, where we would find the people more talkative and demonstrative. On the way there we picked up a hitch-hiker who thanked Sylvia for the ride with a kiss of the hand.

The road to the border lay directly south and along the angry Tisza into Szeged. The river cuts a warning through this attractive city, and the inhabitants live in permanent dread of it. In 1879 the Tisza broke its banks and washed away the entire town centre. Canals were then dug, the river straightened and protective walls constructed, but time and again the waters won. At the first signs of danger the whole population is enrolled to fill sandbags. Szeged was rebuilt from scratch late in the nineteenth century – houses, churches, town hall and all. Thus monuments to national heroes antedating the modern era are rare.

Ask at the local tourist bureau about the principal sights and they will reply: 'Go to the synagogue.' Besides Jerusalem I know of only one other city noteworthy for its synagogue: El Paso in Texas. The Jews gave its eminent architect his head there, with the most astonishing result. Eisenshtat's design endowed the structure with a giant elongated pyramid, perhaps Aztec inspired, though more like a mountain sliced by an earthquake.

In Szeged the synagogue is less a place of worship today than an elaborate echo chamber – another painful reminder of the eclipse of a people who had in their day given sparkle to the arts of their beloved though unappreciative motherland. By an irony, the great cupola is crowned with a Shield of David still illuminated at night. Its architect-rabbi had drawn inspiration from Notre Dame and Chartres, in the hope of emulating their glory. Sylvia and I lingered in the beautiful synagogue, in homage to those who had worshipped there before departing on their train journey for Auschwitz.

Across the Romanian border the people still considered themselves Magyar. We were destined for Arad, or so we thought. A room at the hotel there could be secured only by a supplementary payment and on the understanding we leave promptly the next morning for Oradea, a town some 50 miles to the north. Our bookings had apparently overlapped. It was to be gathered from a heated exchange on the telephone between the hotel clerks of Arad and Oradea, conducted in Hungarian, that it was all the fault of tourist headquarters in Bucharest. Everything wrong in Romania was blamed on someone in Bucharest. I heard the name of Nicolae Ceauşescu, the Great Benefactor and Sage, cursed in an undertone time and again.

Thankfully, the language, of the Romance family, did not completely befuddle, as did Hungarian. Sort out the meaning of a few common prepositions and you can at least divine enough to prevent driving against traffic in one-way streets, and recognise the difference between an ice-cream advertisement and a poster notifying a film programme. More may be decoded by recalling that Romanian attaches the definite article as a suffix to the noun.

Save its southern regions, the country is mostly mountainous. The driving proved more difficult even than in Hungary, and Sylvia was suffering agonies from insect bites collected at humid Szeged. This resulted in an atmosphere between us which husbands and wives create for themselves at least once on every holiday – a depression, unwarranted and illogical. It notifies itself by long ponderous silences. Our Triumph gave the impression of being in similar mood. The car, not one of the more recent models, had behaved dutifully for nearly two thousand miles hitherto but now emitted a protest in the form of a constant rattle, issuing from its innards. I surrendered to my customary defeatism whenever a problem, however slight, rears a mechanical head.

Having been thoroughly trained by the military, Sylvia had once mastered every aspect of the behaviour of motor-car engines. I demanded a diagnosis. This infuriated my wife. She had, years before, deliberately unlearned all her acquired knowledge of internal combustion mysteries, a self-imposed form of amnesia incomprehensible to me. She simply resolved to do nothing with motor cars except drive them. Unnerved, I now anticipated disaster: breakdown in the Carpathians, abandonment of the vehicle while I stumbled on a telephone for assistance from the Romanian version of the AA. I worried whether my insurance policy covered such an eventuality. Was our tour to be suddenly brought to an ignoble halt with a humiliating flight back to London? Who in Romania possessed spare parts for a UK manufactured Triumph, not one of the great international marques? This line of thought, I believe, has come to be known as 'the worst case scenario'.

My wife sullenly usurped the wheel and gently coaxed the car, its rattle now a menacing threnody, into Oradea. We found a garage. As she drove in the mechanics dropped their tools and stared, as if in disbelief. Apparently until this moment they had never observed a woman driving with a grown male in the passenger seat. In a group, the garage hands lifted the bonnet and investigated the cause of my panic, a mere broken connection to some important piping. A repair was improvised on the spot and, refusing payment, they ushered us out. From that moment we resolved never to criticise Romania again, not for mixing up our hotel bookings nor for their obstacle-strewn roads; but to concede generously that, given the difference in mores and the characteristics of the régime, and the poverty, they were a pretty decent lot. This helped.

Desperate to stimulate tourism, Romania had presented us in London with coupons for 44 gallons of petrol at a substantial discount. A further happy discovery accompanied our hotel registration once our itinerary was correctly achieved. At each resting place we were passed an envelope with money in the local currency; they were literally paying us for visiting. There was point to their madness. The sums allocated allowed the tourist, booked in for full board, to eat wherever he chose, a thoughtful gesture indeed. Thus we were able to wander among the people in a fashion denied in Hungary. Moreover by occasionally patronising the stand-up 'people's restaurants', we actually turned a profit on the transaction, with lei in surplus for museums, postcards and tips. Doubtless such concessions are now a joy of the past.

Bucharest can by no flight of imagination be described as pleasing to the eye. In fact it recalled for me the East End of London before Nazi attention scooped chunks out of the district. Bucharest is unexciting, but redeems itself on the periphery with spacious parks, which embrace exquisite flower beds, tranquil lakes and bird life of great variety. We savoured every aspect of Herastrau Park, situated in the northern part of the town. However, a caveat: on the principle that anything Western Europe does badly Eastern Europe can do worse, a most enjoyable afternoon meandering through the park's shady lanes was almost ruined by a demon chorus of heavy rock music from ghetto-blasting radios. It was as though no good Communist citizen would dream of entering this delightful oasis except to demonstrate the superiority of his sound system. The public wandered with their apparatus shoulder high; they rested, radios still blaring, on park benches; they grouped in coveys to compare makes and judge decibel effect. A monumental Lenin stood guard at the entrance to Herastrau Park. Did I detect a reproof on his expression for being rendered stone deaf?

We found the park deserted on 23 August, the national day during Romania's Communist orientation. There was good reason: the desire (if that is the word) of the nation to pay tribute and express gratitude to its own latter-day Lenin, Man of the Century Ceaușescu. That morning we found everyone on the move – men, women and children, all carrying paper flowers and streaming across town to a central square the size of four football pitches. The leader was due to appear on the balcony of the Communist Party citadel monopolising one side of the square.

Having observed the Pope from St Peter's Square, and seen our queen on the balcony of Buckingham Palace saluting her subjects below, we were keen to witness this revolutionary version of mass emotion. It was not to be. We had failed to rise early enough for the occasion and could not find a suitable point of vantage. The populace already overspilled to adjacent thoroughfares, so the adulation proceeded without these two unofficial representatives of the United Kingdom. As night drew on, Bucharest assumed the *en fête* character of Bastille Day in Paris, with enticements of food and drink offered the revellers at every corner.

I had no intention of leaving Romania without some personal memento of the Great One, and found in a bookshop a collection of his writings in English. It was a handsomely bound volume at giveaway price, but I succumbed particularly to its title. The book was unambiguously called *Romania on the Way of Building up the Multilaterally Developed Socialist Society*. In retrospect, the perfidy of crowd hysteria warrants a mention. One day Ceauşescu and his consort, hand in hand, would become the crumpled bodies that made a Bucharest firing squad famous.

The Romania of 1971 gave the diligent wayfarer considerable opportunity to test his historical knowledge, for parts of the country have changed ownership and régime so frequently this past century that many cities are not absolutely certain what they should be called. We spent a couple of days high in a ski resort near Brasov, donning thick sweaters at last. For a period Brasov flourished as Orasul Stalin, the Romanian version of Stalingrad. During the Habsburg zenith it was Brassó (its Hungarian form) but simultaneously Kronstadt for everyone else. Bratislava in Czechoslovakia had not been immune: Hungarians called the place Pozsony but it appeared on many maps as Pressburg. At Cluj in Transylvania, a university town where two opera companies, one Hungarian, the other Romanian, perform, we heard the place referred to as Kolozsvar and Klausenberg also. It all depended on the age and disposition of the speaker.

Since we have now entered the epoch of a redefined St Petersburg, there can be no telling of the problems facing cartographers by this epidemic of name-changing. Hero worship inclines Tel-Aviv to grant every departing worthy immortality with a street name. Elsewhere, airports are used similarly. What's in a name? George Orwell, whose eye for risible possibilities made Britain Airstrip One, would doubtless have found much satirical scope in Eastern Europe's excavation of its buried memories.

Resting at Cluj, we patronised a student café and heard how the young yearned for travel, above all to France, with which Romanians feel a sisterhood. 'Have you no hope for getting away for a while?' I asked.

They told us: 'Only by winning a place in some team, football perhaps. That way we can meet students in other socialist countries. You have to be really outstanding for a tour of the West.' One of them belonged to a folk dancing group that had brought him a trip to East Germany. Apart from the absence of foreign travel, they voiced no complaints. How much did they know, we wondered, of their fellow-students of western vintage, the hairy protesters who in 1971 rejected discipline, boycotted classes and assumed occupation of college premises night and day – militant at home, pacifist abroad? Did Romanian students charge their elders with betrayal of their generation?

Romanians substituted other preoccupations, born of their existence astride the axis of Tatar, Byzantine, Turkish, Hungarian, Austrian and Russian conquest. The country comprises a bewildering conglomeration of ethnic resentments, now back with us today in their startling familiarity. Sylvia and I recall the embittered custodian of the German church in Prejmer, ten miles drive from Brasov through a Carpathian pass. The entire village is built in circular pattern, a fortress community. The official Communist guidebook told of its agricultural co-operative, its cloth-weaving factory and trout-breeding pools, but of the most distinctive feature of the village, its German population settled there for several centuries yet still speaking their native language, not a word. The pastor, in escorting us through the village, lamented their inability to obtain an exit permit for a mere visit, let alone emigration, to Germany.

Doubtless all this, since the Gorbachev era, reads like ancient history. Certainly the curiosity of the only living Yiddish theatre in Europe, at Bucharest, made for a fitting conclusion to our tour. We attended the half-empty theatre for a play by Sholem Aleichem, the sardonic yarn spinner comparable, some claim, to Dickens. The audience availed itself of automatic translation equipment as aid to comprehension.

Backstage, we spoke with the lady administrator of the theatre, whose English would not have disgraced a denizen of Brooklyn. 'We have our own writers, artistes, carpenters, wardrobe staff', she explained. 'And some gentile actors in the company who have learned Yiddish in order to join us. Altogether 130 people in regular employment.'

'Surely it's a luxury for this poor country, when you cater for so minute an audience?'

'The government wants a Yiddish theatre. It's got a Yiddish theatre.'

I wonder where they are now, those 130 in regular employment. Romania has dropped its mask and may well dispense with such flamboyant exercises in token toleration of ethnic diversity. How quiet flows the Danube today?

13 • Connecting Life-lines

In the spring of 1988 I was finalising my book, *The Burning Bush*, published later that year in London, New York and Milan. The opening of the book concerned the life, as far as it is known, of that Jew described as Jesus of Nazareth. My narrative then searched out the Jewish situation in the Ancient and Mediaeval worlds. Its conclusion discussed the conflicts of identity besetting all humanity today. Above all, the book was intended to bring the reader into a closer relationship with the enormity of the Holocaust. My own experience of that period began with my incarceration as a German prisoner of war for three years, 1942 until 1945.

After the end of the Second World War, few spoke of Jewry's tribulations in the terms of a holocaust. The expression came into general parlance in the later 1960s, particularly through the writings of the survivor Elie Wiesel. I am referring now to that earlier era, when I had been thrown together with a Jewish soldier from Palestine, like myself captured by the *Wehrmacht* while serving in the British Eighth Army.

This man, Berthold Sud, originally from Czechoslovakia, remains to this day one of my closest friends. I lost sight of him early in 1945 when we were shunted off to different prison camps. He was subsequently brought to England by our military authorities while I was detained on the Continent by my American liberators a little while longer. Then, when I too reached Britain, I was able to present Berthold to my family, and especially to my wife Sylvia from whom I had been separated for four years. We spent much time with Berthold, together enjoying the delights of London. Sylvia and I hoped he would find a wife here, but this did not materialise, and he was eventually demobilised in Jerusalem, where he intended to spend the rest of his life.

During our detention in 'the bag', as we called it, I remember Berthold being constantly called upon to write letters for some of those who had enlisted with him in Palestine and who were captured with him in the Balkans. This intake included many Jews of Oriental families whose speech in those days was most commonly Arabic. Berthold usually made up their letters into a simple Hebrew.

He enjoyed this activity, for he was fluent in several languages. He could speak and write German, Yiddish, Russian and English, together with his own Czech and Hebrew. It followed, therefore, that he was able to help me develop a considerable knowledge of German, Yiddish and Hebrew – no small aid to my aspiration to launch out as a writer.

In one of our camps, close to the great complex of Auschwitz, we were brought to work daily in a large railway yard where we military captives could observe other kinds of prisoners – mostly civilian Poles, Ukrainians and Jews. The last category were the only ones kept as slaves. They could be seen dropping in their tracks, then carried away by their own comrades never to be encountered again. It was a sight that brought us, for the first time, knowledge of the anguish of Jewish existence on the continent of Europe. Yet how could we begin to imagine the slaughter in progress. This intelligence would require the presence of the allied armies in the area, and that was still months away.

A certain day in our captivity had another interest for us. It was the day following 20 July 1944, the momentous attempt on Hitler's life at his military headquarters in East Prussia. Our working party – I was present as medical orderly – began spreading word of the Führer's demise, bringing with it the release of every single prisoner. Berthold clambered on to a girder and called out: 'Careful, chaverim [comrades], and don't be so sure.'

Our jailors announced that Hitler had saved himself. He had

spoken on the radio that very morning, they said. The conspirators, the guards informed us, had all been captured. Interestingly, we were able in our camp to obtain German newspapers, which Berthold and a few others among us could read like natives. That night, we prisoners knew as much as our guards.

Hitler was still in command of most of Europe. True, he had sustained injuries with the near success of the conspiracy, and soon some brave men would be brought to trial and condemned to death. It even happened that three of our own number started to run off, believing they could escape. But of course nothing came of it. The three were picked up within an hour and locked away.

As already noted, a good proportion of those captured with my friend Berthold Sud in Greece and Crete in 1941 were youngsters of the Oriental Jewish community in Palestine. They had already been through a hellish time while I was still taking things fairly easy with my unit in Somerset waiting for our moment of departure for the East. Those Jews of Palestine, I was to discover, were particularly impressed by one sergeant captured with them. He was the leader of the camp when I joined them in 1943. The sergeant bore the name of Josef Krellenbaum. Originating in Poland, Krellenbaum had lived in Palestine since 1930, and certainly knew how to keep spirits up in our camp. Most of us held Sergeant Krellenbaum in high regard. His peacetime activity was as trade union organiser in the port of Haifa. We looked on him as one of the leaders of the Jewish population in Palestine, while he himself regarded his fellow Palestinian prisoners as the cream of the British Army. And why not! It made them feel quite proud of themselves.

Outsider that I was, I grew impressed at the way Krellenbaum cared for his fellows. On returning to his Haifa home at the end of hostilities he changed his name, which meant coral tree, into its Hebrew form of Almogi. He did indeed reach the top in Palestine's trade union organisation. When the State of Israel was established in 1948 he gained a place in parliament as one of Prime Minister Ben-Gurion's most effective disciples. He reached Cabinet rank in Ben-Gurion's various governments, and later he was appointed head of the Jewish Agency, the worldwide organisation that partnered Israel in adjusting newly arrived immigrants as citizens. In our prison days he was also accepted as spokesman by the German officers with whom he came into contact, and they called upon him to march his people out of Lamsdorf Stalag when it appeared the Russians were closing in. Berthold was among those on the march, and suffered terribly from frostbite. It was in the bitter winter weeks early in 1945.

I joined a small British group in Lamsdorf which refused to march. We held out until evacuated by rail. Squeezed into cattle-trucks for five days in the move from Lamsdorf in Poland, we crossed Czechoslovakia to Memmingen in South Germany. On one of the rare occasions we were released from our moving prison to relieve ourselves, an old sweat of a soldier asked me, 'Where are we?' 'There's the Charles Bridge of Prague', I replied. He went on: 'We shall always be able to say we've done our business all over Prague.'

With the ending of hostilities in Europe and the Far East in 1945, the conflicts between Jews and Arabs in Palestine grew into the savagely fought civil war with which we are now so familiar. This of course was not the only such problem in the world, but it was the one which carried much of the pain of Europe's recent past with it. Berthold found himself in the midst of this civil war as a soldier again, this time in the Zionist force, the Haganah. As a consequence, once again, he was unable to engage in any activity to prepare himself for civilian life.

Berthold met his wife Miriam, also from Czechoslovakia, in the Haganah in Jerusalem, where she too was mobilised in the Zionist defence force. They married in a Jerusalem at war, but dreamed of peace for all the inhabitants of the Holy Land. During the Second World War, Miriam enrolled in service with the Jewish Agency, had been sent to Istanbul as a conduit bearing despatches back to Palestine, a task of no small significance in the endeavours to bring more Jews into Palestine. This rescue activity was accepted by almost every western democracy except Britain. The Sud husband-and-wife team gained their military discharge at last when Israel became an independent republic.

Miriam confessed to me, when we first met in 1951 in Tel-Aviv – she and Berthold occupied a single rented room there – that what she missed most in Israel was mountains. She had not seen a mountain since her departure from Czechoslovakia 15 years earlier. She needed to recover that geographical sensation, Miriam said, if she was ever to restore real joy to her existence. She was speaking of a time when Israeli citizens were unable to travel abroad unless their employment made this possible. Such was the situation for a decade and more. Overseas holidays were rare, except for the moneyed few.

I recalled that thought of hers again when our children were teenagers, while Miriam and Berthold were reluctantly resigned to having none of their own. By this time they had made the transition to the United States and were living in Atlanta, Georgia. We drove into the Blue Ridge mountains one day, these two and my wife and me, where I could sense those earlier yearnings Miriam had carried with her in the Middle East.

This story will now wing back to 1938 and the drift of our planet to Armageddon. About the time of Munich, Berthold still lived with his parents in Prague, where his father occupied the pulpit of a small synagogue. The Nazi party in the neighbourhood had ordered the rabbi to enrol his son to prepare a list detailing all the Jews in the region served by his synagogue. The catalogue was duly completed, and delivered as required to the local SS headquarters.

As it happened, Berthold's parents possessed visas for the United States. But though they wanted to remain in Prague and share whatever fate had in store for their children, their son finally persuaded them to depart. He then joined an illegal transport making for Palestine across the Mediterranean. Berthold was picked up in this vessel by the Royal Navy and interned in Palestine – the British custom then.

A Very British Subject

He extricated himself from internment by the usual method of the time, for the war against Germany had already begun and was shifting back and forth in the Libyan desert. Thus he enrolled in the British Army, shortly afterwards finding himself in General Wavell's Middle Eastern campaign, only to be captured in Greece and carried off to spend the rest of the war in the stalags. We first met in one of those stalags two years later, when Berthold found it quite strange that there existed Jews in England like me who had never learned Hebrew and could not make themselves understood either in Yiddish or German.

'You mean you are a married man?' Berthold asked in his idiosyncratic English. 'You can't be old enough. Where I come from they would describe you as a boychik.' Berthold, with my blessing, wrote to my wife in London and asked her to send messages to members of his family, both in the United States and Palestine. He could not say whether any lived on in Hitler's Europe.

Berthold made no reference to a wife or sweetheart of his own in those days. Had there been one? Years later I discovered that his first meeting with Miriam took place at a bus-stop in Jerusalem early in 1947. That city was in desperate straits, with three different races, British, Jewish and Arab, living side by side and unable to agree on almost anything. The British largely took the part of the Arabs, and indeed had every intention of remaining in the area themselves as the most important element for many a year to come. We are, of course, speaking here of the period when Palestine was already divided, a large portion having been absorbed into the kingdom of Jordan.

After their marriage, Berthold and Miriam continued in their Haganah duties until 1948. The first time I met them together was when they set up house in that miniscule room in Tel-Aviv. One night their radio was stolen from their room. That instrument had provided them with the only recreation in their lives – music. It was the last straw, for they could not afford to replace it. Miriam had already explained to Berthold how much she pined for change, for the sight of mountains, and now they were even deprived of the joy of listening to music. This was a time of hardship for the mass of ordinary working people in Israel, and Miriam now declared she had given all she could of herself to the homeland of the Jews.

And so we meet them again in the United States, ensconced in their far from lavish two-room apartment in Atlanta, Georgia. Berthold went back to his law studies there and achieved a good degree. Yet the only suitable work he could find in Atlanta, not yet a US citizen, was as sales assistant in a department store owned by an old Prague congregant of his father's. Miriam fared better, because she was able to resume her occupation practised in Czechoslovakia – as a scientific laboratory expert. And so we find the Suds at home in the USA well before the great migrations of East Europeans to that country during the Carter and Reagan presidencies.

Because of the injuries sustained on that long march westward from the stalag, Berthold has been a British Army pensioner ever since, though the sums paid have contracted over the years. He has often spoken with pride at being an Eighth Army veteran. He uses much of his spare time now in a labour of love in the hospitals of his latest American domicile, in Hendersonville, North Carolina. He is much appreciated by patients and visitors, often serving them that local speciality, the BLT. The abbreviation is commonly accepted for a dressed-up sandwich of bacon, lettuce and tomato. He offers this delicacy many times a day, though Berthold himself could never allow bacon to pass his lips.

Hendersonville falls into the Bible belt in America and has taken these two to its heart. Berthold is a synagogue member frequently required to officiate at religious services; is he not a rabbi's son? And for Miriam, too, synagogue affairs are a very significant part of existence. Fate decided it this way. Had they been blessed with children of their own in Israel, I have no doubt Berthold and Miriam would have remained there. It was not to be. Perhaps the kindest as well as the most erudite man I ever came close to, Berthold has never been employed in any labour beyond the use of his own hands. He was compelled to leave the Jewish homeland at the height of his powers for another country where he could graduate as a lawyer but he was unable to utilise his knowledge. Never bitter, never angry, he and Miriam have grown to love America and its people. Doubtless they often think of their past life, their childhood in Czechoslovakia, their growing maturity in that old Palestine which became modern Israel, and all the friends and relatives they left behind. President Clinton will never invite them to a reception in the White House, though he could meet no finer American citizens than my friends, the Suds.

Within my own family circle there are several writers of one kind or another. But here I wish to speak of one who has published nothing, nor made his mark in any other public manner. He is my brother Jack.

A brother in Israel's 1948 War of Independence

This brother had an experience in 1948, when he was a young man of 22 beginning to feel his strength, that made him different from the man he might have become. This experience propelled him into tasks of a kind he had previously tackled as a wireless and radar specialist in the Royal Air Force.

I was unaware of brother Jack's involvement in certain events I would discuss seven years later in my biography of David Ben-Gurion. Another 40 years needed to elapse before Jack opened up to me of the part he played in the sinking of a small naval craft in the Mediterranean. He was the only one of our mother's nine children absent at the marriage that summer of 1948 of our elder brother Pinchas. The ceremony took place at a synagogue in the East London area of Dalston. Our mother had died aged 54 a year earlier, and Jack was now abroad for reasons of his own.

Another brother, one of the younger boys, made an announcement at that wedding: 'You don't seem to know about it, but Jack's in Palestine fighting with the Jews.' But what he was actually engaged in we had no way of knowing. Jack returned home late in that same year and had little to report on how he had spent his time among the people of the new nation of Israel. While in the RAF he had been located in various stations in the Middle East, but never in what was then known as Palestine.

Now the situation there was vastly changed. As one of a small group of volunteers, Jack was engaged yet again in radar, but this time to protect the few planes and vessels of the nascent Israeli armed forces. On that summer's day in 1948, when the Jewish state was only a few weeks old, Jack was doing all he could, together with his comrades, to place one of these radar stations on the Tel-Aviv shore.

The work was stopped suddenly, and Jack was ordered to join a well-armed detachment preparing to clamber aboard a pleasure boat at the sea shore. They were then to be towed out – barely a couple of hundred yards – to sea, thence to make a bee-line for a vessel just beyond. This vessel was the *Altalena*, one of the landing craft employed by the American forces in the assault on Europe four years before.

The name *Altalena* had been the literary pseudonym of the acclaimed leader of the right wing in Zionism, the Revisionist party – Vladimir Jabotinsky. He had died in 1940 in the United States. The party was subsequently commanded by Menachem Begin, a man Ben-Gurion refused in those days to recognise as a Zionist leader with any rights in the country where he, Ben-Gurion, served as Prime Minister. Members of Begin's *Irgun Zvai Leumi* had brought the *Altalena* across the seas. It carried 5,000 rifles and 250 machine guns.

Begin's was a private army, and my brother Jack had no intention of deserting the government's side to join it, as had some of the British boys. For that matter, neither did Berthold go over to Begin's people in Jerusalem. In fact, Ben-Gurion demanded of the dissenters the surrender of their troops and arms to the army controlled by his own – legitimate – party of the left. Ironically, Begin was destined himself to become Prime Minister of Israel in 1977, not only defeating the left-wing Mapai party, but going on to make peace with Egypt.

My brother Jack (properly Gerald) Levy was born into that

younger section of our family fathered by Solly Levy. Jack regarded himself as fully trained in radar, and engaged as such with a few others like himself, British, South African and American. I discovered subsequently that his and their expertise was not so profound, and that the Israelis themselves had not a single specialist of their own with experience in this field.

So there was my brother and his comrades offshore in the Mediterranean, not far from the last radar station they had put into operation. Soon, they were aboard the *Altalena*. According to Jack's account, they had climbed on to the vessel just two or three hours before it went under. He had been called upon to cut through the *Altalena*'s electronics and collect as much of it as possible to transport to the beach.

Meanwhile the beach area was crowded with personnel belonging to both Jewish factions – the official force opposed by Begin's men. In the midst of it all, Jack and his detachment were working frantically to gain possession of the all-important equipment.

Eventually, Ben-Gurion ensured that a United Nations cease-fire would be honoured. Begin himself had been on board the *Altalena*. He and his followers mostly managed to escape Ben-Gurion's grasp. The vessel went under, complete with its weaponry. Earlier, emissaries from both sides had failed to reach agreement on the destination of the arms on board. Now, all such was lost, with the exception of the radar saved from the doomed ship.

After the scuttling of the *Altalena*, the possibility of mutiny by certain units of the government forces was halted, though 14 soldiers, mainly members of the *Irgun*, lost their lives. Begin succeeded in his escape and continued his struggle, chiefly in the Jerusalem hills, where my friend Berthold was active in one of Ben-Gurion's formations.

To my knowledge, Berthold and my brother Jack never met, neither then nor afterwards. Jack has never made a return visit to Israel, nor has he ever taken part in any veterans' gathering of his volunteer group, the *Machal*.

One of the volunteers working together with Jack was the

young Britisher Vidal Sassoon. He also returned to London to open a ladies hairdressing salon, while Jack utilised his knowledge of electronics in the manufacture of television equipment. Vidal Sassoon, who has often made a pilgrimage to the Jewish state, finally made his home and fortune among the film colony of Los Angeles. His many acquaintances there include a host of former Israelis now domiciled in California.

Yet Jack's Israel experience was kept his own secret. He could never speak of Jews as being Zionists or non-Zionists. He hardly thinks of this people, of which he is so definitely a part, as having any characteristics special to themselves. Nor did he see the Arabs as antagonists, even though some wished to drive the Jews out. Religion is a subject he cannot bring himself to attach to any group of human beings. They are all just people to Jack, and he has affinity with them all.

In the early 1960s when travel to the Soviet empire was almost impossible for tourists, Jack drove across Europe and managed to reach Odessa. He hoped for a discovery relating to our mother's young life there. But what he found held no significance regarding our family's past. Jack returned to London a disappointed traveller. Doubtless a younger generation of the family exists in various parts of the world, yet still unknown to the rest of us.

Out of Trinity College, Dublin

As a teenager in Dublin, my wife Sylvia was connected with a group of youngsters who included Myer Herman, a student of medicine at Trinity College. This quiet lad came into my ken much later, however, during my first visit to Dublin in the late 1930s. Myer was hoping to win the charms of Sylvia's closest friend, Bea Brennan, but nothing grew from this. Bea was a beauty, while Myer could not conceal his rather unassuming personality.

After he graduated as a doctor Myer came to London, while Bea lived on in Dublin determined to find a real prince charming. To one such she was eventually married and they set up home in hospitable Canada. Sylvia's family had returned to England a few years earlier, with herself gaining an excellent post, referred to earlier, on a London newspaper. She was at the old *Daily Sketch* still when I fled my humble clerical duties at the London Gas Company to live in Paris and try to fulfil my ambition as a writer.

But I was home again, not yet having achieved that ambition, on the outbreak of war in September 1939, and not gainfully employed. And neither was Myer Herman. He would sleep in the homes of his friends while awaiting acceptance into the British Army's medical corps. Well, here was Myer in London, seeking me out early one morning, at Euston Station. He had slept rough that night. I was about to take a train into the country to where my youngest brothers had been evacuated with their Hackney elementary school. Myer desperately needed a small loan to transport him to the War Office and an interview there. I proffered a coin, enough to enable him to obtain some breakfast and pay his fare to Whitehall.

Within a week or so, what a transformation took place! There stood a First Lieutenant cutting a dash as a medical officer in the RAMC, furthering the needs of a battalion of the West Kents. It transpired that Lt Myer Herman received a posting to France with his regiment when I was already ensconced over there as a private soldier in a field ambulance unit. We both came through Dunkirk with the British Expeditionary Force and were soon made ready again to be sent around the globe whenever the top brass so decided.

For both of us this proved to be the Middle East battle zone; medical officer Herman with the infantry and Private Litvinoff with his ambulance unit. Only after the war did I discover that Myer had taken a staff car near El Alamein up the Blue, as we referred to the desert, to find me and my ambulance section. He did indeed reach my unit, but too late – for Private Litvinoff had already been gathered up as a prisoner of war.

Myer himself caught a German shell at Alamein. The wound kept him out of action for a while. The army raised his rank and decorated him for his good works after a spell in

Alexandria. It then took him out of this firing line altogether. He subsequently returned to 'Blighty' and obtained whatever news of my fate known then by Sylvia. Myer brought a modicum of comfort to all his friends in England, especially to the families of my wife and myself. Sylvia had by now begun her own military service. Myer, well at last, was posted to Burma, to join General Bill Slim's formations against the Japanese.

The man was totally dedicated to the practice of medicine, and experienced fulfilment as a doctor no matter where he found himself. He reached this fulfilment after the war in the Third World. An assignment to care for the health of his own people came to him from North Africa. He thus found himself back in the lands he recalled from his army days. Mostly, he would be treating the poorer members of the Jewish community in Morocco. There Myer found an organisation of which he had never previously heard, the Hassidim known as 'Lubavitch', that brought religious exactitude together with love, schooling and food to the deprived.

Following a year in Morocco, he discovered this sect again in Iran, nurturing the slum populations of the Mellahs. In both countries Myer was sponsored by well-established American charities. Once, Sylvia and I went over to Paris especially to spend time with Myer, who was attending a conference of Third World practitioners in the science of human care.

Myer's career now reached a happy development through his marriage to Ida, a girl who had spent the war years as a Wren, the British Navy's women's section. Sylvia and I were chosen as their officiating couple at the synagogue, a very modest structure in those days, in the London borough of Chelsea. Circumstances then took him to New England to the state of Massachusetts, to succour other people in need. He and his wife took Boston in their stride. 'Why here'? I asked Myer while on a visit to the United States. He replied: 'No other doctor in this state wanted the job. And as I have no wish or intention to go into private practice, the position was ideal for a Jewish fellow from Dublin.'

A Very British Subject

At home in Lexington with their two young sons, Myer and Ida retained their British citizenship. A neighbour was the political and linguistic writer Noam Chomsky of Harvard University. But the Hermans were the ones with the cheapest automobile in town; it carried the insignia of the state of Massachusetts, and also served as an ambulance when required. The Hermans and the Chomskys could be found at the same liberal synagogue in Lexington. It was presided over by Sefton Temkin, the Anglo-Jewish scholar who for a period ministered to this congregation.

Myer and Ida returned to the United Kingdom from time to time, in addition to visits to Israel in that period when the Jewish state gathered the goodwill of the entire democratic world into its welcoming arms. Myer's sons were proudest of their father for all he had accomplished under British military service. He concluded his working life in the United States at Bridgeport, Connecticut, with our own association continuing until Myer's health gave out, at last, just a few years ago.

His entire medical career since leaving the armed forces had been devoted to the poorest of the poor. In North Africa he had given himself particularly to those who hoped one day to reach the shores of Israel. In America he was consulted most frequently by the black population, which took this Jew from Dublin to its heart. There is a lady now alone in Vancouver who must think of Myer Herman much as we do in London. She is that other Dubliner whom he had once hoped to make his own.

Each of the three people discussed in these final pages affected the author in making his way in the world. Each of them placed himself, as it were, into the development of the narrative. Circumstances had taken all four of us into battle zones that are now part of the history of our times. Judaism also takes its place in that history, for Judaism demanded to be recognised as our common denominator. Readers will perhaps find their own connecting links in the life-lines of those who appear in this section of the book.